HOW TO TALK BOWLING

HOW TO TALK BOWLING

by Dawson Taylor

Illustrated by Taylor Jones

Dembner Books • New York

Dembner Books
Published by Red Dembner Enterprises Corp., 80 Eighth Avenue, New York, N.Y. 10011
Distributed by W. W. Norton & Company, Inc., 500 Fifth Avenue, New York, N.Y. 10110

Library of Congress Cataloging in Publications Data

Taylor, Dawson.
    How to talk bowling.

    Includes index.
    1. Bowling.   I. Title.
GV903.T33   1987   794.6   86-29178
ISBN 0-934878-85-4 (pbk.)

To Barbara Jones and Ingrid Palm,
who have boxes of bowling trophies in their basements.

And to Mary Ellen Taylor,
who was always on the sidelines cheering.

CONTENTS

FOREWORD

It gives me great pleasure to write this introduction to *How To Talk Bowling* by Dawson Taylor and Taylor Jones. I am also very pleased that I have been selected as one of the well-known bowlers whose career is discussed.

Bowling, like all other sports, has a language of its own. The sport of bowling has been rolling along for more than one hundred years in the United States. If you happen to read a report of bowling in the early 1900s you will find that in those days the bowlers ran into "railroads," that is, wide-open splits, just as the bowlers of today do.

In order to enjoy bowling to its fullest extent, I recommend that every bowler familiarize himself or herself with this "lexicon of bowling." It will add tremendously to the pleasure of your participation in this great sport.

Earl Anthony

INTRODUCTION

In 1985 in the United States about 68 million people bowled at 8,629 bowling establishments with 159,394 lanes. This indoor sport, also called ten pins, is played in Canada, Japan, Scandinavia, Mexico, Australia, Central and South America as well.

Bowling has a history that goes back many years. It has been traced to the tomb of an Egyptian child of 5200 B.C. where archeologists found nine pieces of stone, presumably to be set up as pins, and a stone "ball." The ball had to be rolled at the pins through an archway consisting of three pieces of marble. In the Italian Alps about 2000 years ago, the tossing of stones underhand at a stationary object was supposed to be the beginnings of bocce, still played in Italy. The Polynesians also played a game using pins and balls of stone. They rolled the stone ball a distance of sixty feet, the same length as that of a modern ten-pin bowling lane.

Bowling at pins originated in ancient Germany. There, during the third or fourth century A.D., it is believed that certain religious rites evolved into the sport of bowling. Parishioners placed their kegels, clubs carried for self-protection and sport, at one end of a long lane. The kegels represented the *Heide,* the heathen. A stone was rolled at the *Heide,* and those who successfully toppled them were believed to have cleansed themselves of sin.

This religious practice lasted less than two centuries, but the activity persisted as a pastime. Eventually nobility took it up as a game. The peasant's club evolved into bowling pins. To this day bowlers are referred to as Keglers.

The game changed over the centuries. The stone ball rolled at the pins became larger and eventually was replaced by a wooden ball. In the fourteenth century the game was played with three pins in some areas and with a many as seventeen in others. During the fifteenth, sixteenth, and seventeenth centuries, the game spread from Germany into Holland, Austria, and Switzerland. The playing surface varied. Generally it was either hard-packed cinders or clay. The first roofed-over lanes were used in London around 1455 and that was the true beginning of modern bowling as an all-weather, around-the-clock game.

Many rulers frowned on the game because they felt the players should practice their archery instead. In 1388 King Richard II of England prohibited the game, which was also criticized because it had become a source of gambling.

In 1511 King Henry VIII issued an edict declaring, "the game of bowles is an evil because all the alleys are in operation in conjunction with saloons, or dissolute places, and bowling has ceased to be a sport, and rather a form of vicious gambling."

Other prominent historical figures took a much more favorable view of the game. Martin Luther built a bowling lane for the young people in his family. And there is the famous anecdote about Sir Francis Drake, who, in 1588, did not allow reports of the approaching Spanish Armada to interrupt his bowling game. Drake told his scouts who brought him the news that there was time left for him to score some more strikes of his own and still strike down the Spaniards. He did both.

It is believed that pin bowling was introduced in America in 1623 by the Dutch settlers on Manhattan Island. The game, called nine pins, was played outdoors with nine pins and a ball. The British version of this game was called skittles. In skittles the players roll or throw a ball or a flat disc, called a cheese, at the nine skittles at the end of a 21-foot lane and score a point for each skittle knocked down. Nine pins were set up in a diamond formation and knocking all the pins down with the first throw was a prime objective.

Nine pins became very popular not only as a sport, but as a bettor's game. The Puritans outlawed bowling because of the gambling. Later in 1841, the Connecticut state legislature prohibited the game and other states soon did the same.

Then a devoted bowler figured out a way around the prohibition. He

added a tenth pin. The game, renamed ten pins, quietly resumed and
became more and more popular. By the middle of the nineteenth
century the first indoor lanes were built in big cities such as New York,
Syracuse, Buffalo, Cincinnati, and Milwaukee.

Although there was growing enthusiasm for the game, it was inhibited
by the lack of standard rules and equipment. In 1875 an attempt was
made to standardize the game and bring it under the control of one
ruling body. It took twenty years for this to happen, but finally, on
September 9, 1895, the American Bowling Congress was organized in
New York City. Rules and equipment were developed—and adhered
to—and the game has remained basically unchanged since then, except
for the technological advancements brought on by the modern age.
These include the introduction of automatic pinsetters and plastics and
other synthetic materials.

Once the ABC was established, bowling's popularity began to grow at
a remarkable pace. The first ABC bowling tournament was conducted
January 8-11, 1901, on the second floor of the Wellstock Building on
Wabash Avenue in Chicago. Six lanes and a set of bleachers were
installed. The lanes were christened by officials of the ABC who rolled
the first balls down each lane. Not one of them made a strike. The
tournament continued with play from 3:30 P.M. to midnight each day.
Forty-one teams rolled 78 doubles and 115 single matches. The crowd
in the bleachers was large and rowdy. The newspaper reports of the day
said, "The noise made by the spectators would put a bleacher delega-
tion at a baseball game to shame."

The first ABC champions were the Chicago Standard team, who won
the 5-man event with a score of 2720 (a 181 average per man). Frank
Bull was singles and all-events champion with 633 (a 211 average) and
1736 (193 average) respectively. The prize money, $1,592, was paid in
gold.

In 1916 forty women met in a bowling alley in St. Louis, Missouri, to
compete in the first national women's bowling tournament. After that
initial match they organized a national women's association intended to
promote bowling among women throughout the country. That 40-member
fledgling organization grew during the next seven decades. Today the

Women's International Bowling Congress has about 4,200,000 members. The male counterpart, the ABC, today has about 4,800,000.

From the early 1900s until the early part of the 1940s, bowling pins were set by hand. Then came the introduction of semi-automatic pinsetters. These were slotted racks suspended above the lanes. When the pins were placed into the racks, the human operator lowered the entire ten pin set-up at once. After the ball was rolled, he removed the fallen pins.

In 1944 bowling was revolutionized by the automatic pinsetting machine. American Machine and Foundry Company bought the new patent for the machine, which used two complete sets of pins, one set for the first ball, another for the second or spare ball. The machine was equipped with a sweep bar that removed all the wood on the lane after the first ball had been rolled, but memorized the position of the pins left standing, if any. Then it assembled the pins mechanically into a rack above the lane. When all the pins were in their proper places the rack automatically lowered them to the surface of the lane setting only those previously standing pins, and then retreated. If a strike had been made, all the pins would be released in their proper spots.

The new automatic pinsetters soon were installed in every bowling lane in the country. No longer did the lane operators have to depend upon pin boys. The pay was low in those days, about five cents a game when a game cost 35 cents. It was hard to persuade anyone to take the late night/early morning shifts.

The advent of plastic changed other aspects of bowling. Pins were originally made of maple, a hard wood. Now they are made of plastic and outlast wooden pins many times over. Plastic covered bowling lanes are easier to maintain. Plastic balls hold their shape better and longer.

It wasn't until 1958 that a professional bowlers organization was formed. Instigated by a bright attorney, Eddie Elias of Akron, Ohio, a charter group of 33 members was formed. Today the Professional Bowlers Association has grown to nearly 2900 members who bowl for prize money of more than $3,000,000. The PBA bowling tour was first presented on television in 1962 and is one of the longest running sports programs on television.

Considering the millions of active men and women bowlers in the United States and the millions who watch the sport on television each week, it can be truly said that the sport of bowling is America's favorite pastime.

1. Earl Anthony 2. Nelson Burton, Jr. 3. Marshall Holman
4. Dave Davis   5. Marion Ladewig 6. Don Carter
7. Wayne Webb 8. George Pappas 9. Larry Laub 10. Carmen Salvino

LEXICON

ABC

n: the American Bowling Congress, the ruling organization of the bowling world. It supervises the sport, establishes standards for the construction of lanes, and determines the specifications of the bowling balls and pins.

alley

n: playing surface, made of maple and pine boards.

all the way

n: finishing a game from any point with nothing but strikes.

anchorman

n: the last man on a five man bowling team. He is usually the best bowler on the team and the one most likely to "lay a foundation" strike in the ninth frame and throw three strikes in the tenth frame to win the game. The term originated in 1913 when Hans Arfsparger bowled in the fifth position on the Anchor Brewing team in Milwaukee. He struck out 94 times in succession in tenth frames. Because of this and the company name he was called the Anchor Man.

angle

n: the direction a bowling ball takes as it enters

(angle cont'd)

the 1~3 pocket on its way to achieving a strike. A proper angle causes the ball to hit the head~pin first and then deflect just enough so that it continues onward through the pins to strike the 5~pin located in the center of the cluster. A bad angle happens when the bowler's ball deflects either to the left or right of the 5~pin.

apple

n: bowling ball. Also applied to a bowl~er who fails to come through in a clutch situation—as in "he got the apple," the dryness in the throat under pressure that makes it difficult to swallow.

Dave Husted

approach

n: the name for the area behind the foul line. It extends fifteen feet and is marked with dowels imbedded in the floor so that the bowler can readily find his same starting position time after time. The bowler is said to "make his approach" to the foul line.

armswing

n: the arc of the bowling arm and hand from the first move toward the line until the delivery of the ball over the line.

arrows

n: the darts which are inset into the surface of the lane to act as guides for the bowler to choose

(arrows cont'd)

his line to the pocket. He may say, "I'm going over the 10~board and if the ball does not come up to the pocket, he may move his line one board in~ward to the 11~board. The boards are counted from the outer or channel side of the lane.

automatic foul detector

n: an electric eye positioned near floor level. The beam is interrupted if the bowler's foot slides across the foul line. It indicates a foul on the bowler by blowing horns and whistles. Bowling stops on the lanes while everyone points the finger at the un~fortunate bowler who fouled. The penalty for fouling is loss of pins scored with that ball.

automatic pinsetter

n: the machine invented in the early 1940s that automatically clears the dead wood and resets the pins. Because of this invention, bowling experienced a tremendous boom. The inventor got a million dollars from A.M.F. Soon after, Brunswick brought out its ver~sion of an automatic pinsetter.

Baby split

n: bowling pins left standing with space for only one intermediate pin between them. A ball cannot go between the pins of a small split. The 3~10 for a righthanded bowler, for a lefthander it is the 2~7. It can be made by fitting the ball between

(baby split cont'd)

the pins, or on the outside by hitting the front pin on the outside so as to knock it into the back pin.

baby split with company

n: the 2~7~8 or 3~9~10 split leave. The 8~pin and the 9~pin are the company.

Anne Marie Pike

baby the ball

vt: to be too delicate and not deliver the ball with authority.

backup

n: a ball that falls away to the right for righthanded bowlers, to the left for lefties.

backup alley

n: a lane that holds or tends to stop a ball from rolling to the pocket.

balk

n: an incomplete approach in which the bowler does not deliver the ball.

vt: to interfere or cause another bowler to stop his approach or not complete it in his normal fashion.

ball return

n: the track between lanes on which the ball makes

(ball return cont'd)

its return trip from the pit after knocking down the pins. Previously the ball return was visible. Modern lanes are constructed with each return in a tunnel centered between two lanes.

barmaid

n: a pin hidden behind another pin.

beer frame

n: in team play, when all but one of the players scores a strike, the one who doesn't must treat. Also any designated frame in a game where the lowest scorer is stuck with drinks for everybody else.

belly the ball

vt: increase the width of a hook from an inside starting angle.

bench work

n: any type of conversation or other actions intended to upset an opponent. Also called bench jockeying.

bender

n: a big curve or hook that travels down the lane close to the channel and then breaks sharply into the pocket.

Rodney Dangerfield

bicycle

n: a hidden pin, same as barmaid.

big ball

n: a working hook that enables a bowler to carry strikes on something less than perfect pocket hits.

big ears

n: the 4~6~7~10. Also called big four.

big fill

n: 9 or 10 pins on a spare or on a double strike.

Chris Schenkel

big five

n: a spare leave of three on one side and two on the other.

blind

n: score allowed for an absent member, usually low, as a penalty.

blocked lanes

n: a condition that occurs when the lane operators illegally apply surface oil or lane conditioners to help the bowler make more strikes or, the reverse, hurt him by making the ball skid more than usual and thus harder to control.

blow

n: a shot for a spare that leaves one or more pins standing—a miss, an error, an open.

blowout

n: downing all the pins but one.

board

n: a lane consists of individual strips of lumber called boards. Pros call them by number, fifth board, fifteenth board, etc., for targeting purposes.

body english

n: contortion of the arms, legs and trunk in a vain attempt to steer the ball after it has left the hand.

bonus

n: pins awarded for winning game in match play bowling, usually 30 or 50.

bowling shoes

n: the specially designed shoes worn by bowlers. The left, the sliding foot, for right-handers, has a slippery, hard sole so that the left foot can slide toward the line. The heel of that shoe is of rubber so that when it comes down on the lane it acts as a brake to keep the bowler from sliding over the foul line. For lefthanders the shoe is on the other foot. The other shoe has

"Toothpick"
Rick Sajek

(bowling shoes cont'd)

a conventional leather or plastic sole but no rubber heel.

break

n: a lucky shot. Also a stopper after a number of consecutive strikes.

break~of~the~ boards

n: the area, twenty feet from the foul line, where the boards are spliced. Bowling lanes are built with hard maple boards for the area immediately beyond the foul line. Then pine boards are joined to them at a point twenty feet down the lane. The doweling of the joint has alternating light and dark boards so they are often called "the piano keys."

Johnny Petraglia

Brooklyn

n: a hit into the wrong pocket. The 1~3 pocket is the strike pocket for a righthander. When the ball crosses over and hits into the 1~2 pocket it is called a Brooklyn or a Brooklyn hit. Another name for it is a Jersey strike. Of course, the 1~3 pocket is the Brooklyn hit for the lefthander. When a Brooklyn hit causes a strike it is called a Brooklyn strike.

broom ball

n: a ball that hits the 1~3 pocket in such a way that the pins scatter as though they were swept with a broom.

bucket

n: the 2~4~5~8 spare leave for a righty; 3~5~6~9 for a lefty. Also called the dinner bucket.

Call the numbers

v: pins left on a spare or split are always called in a definite numerical sequence, the lower numbers first. For example, it is the 4~6~7~10 split not the 4~7~6~10 split.

carry

n: the power in the bowling ball as it strikes the pins. An explosive ball has a lot of carry, knocking down all the pins or most of them.

CC

n: double century or a 200 game.

channel

n: the modern day polite name for what used to be called the gutter. It is the depressed area 9½ inches wide which runs along both sides of the lane.

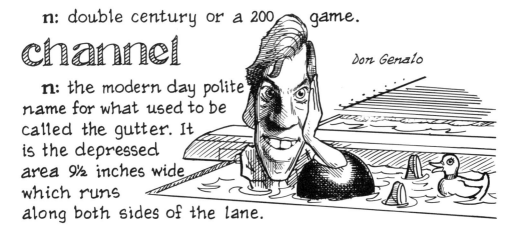

Don Genalo

If a bowler rolls his ball into the channel he scores a zero for that ball. Good bowlers rarely roll gutter balls but recently Don Genalo needed to get three pins out of a five pin spare on his last ball in a PBA tournament to win first prize. He threw his ball into the gutter and it cost him $7500.

charge

n: term used by pros to describe a sensational spurt of high scoring.

Betty Morris

charts

n: charts are the records good bowlers keep on lane conditions. They remind the bowler that certain lanes should be played from an outside angle and others from an inside angle in order to get the highest scores.

cheese cakes

n: lanes on which strikes come easy.

chicken wing

n: a bowler who lets his elbow wander out from his body in his backswing is said to have a chicken wing. It is a bad fault and causes a loss of action on the

(chicken wing cont'd)
ball as it is delivered over the foul line. Also known as a flying elbow.

choke

vt: fail to accomplish objective because of nervousness or fright. Same as "apple."

chop

v: to cut one or more pins out of a spare and leaving one standing. Most frequently the 6~pin is chopped off a 6~10 leave or vice versa. It can happen, too, on other multiple pin spares such as the 1~2~4 where either the 1~pin or 4~pin is left standing.

Christmas tree

n: the 3~7~10 leave for a righthander or 2~7~10 for a lefthander.

Cincinnati

n: the 8~10 split.

clean game

n: no misses or splits—a strike or spare in each of the ten frames.

clothes line

n: the 1~2~4~7 or 1~3~6~10 spare leave.

come up

v: the action of the ball as it nears the pocket. If it has enough side spin it will take off on its own axis and come up into the pocket — the space between the 1 and 3 pins for righthanders, the 1 and 2 for lefthanders.

conversion

n: knocking down with the second ball all the pins that remain. This results in a spare. If there is a split after the first ball is thrown, and the spare is made, one says, "he converted the split."

count

n: number of pins knocked down on first ball of each frame.

cracked thumb

n: many bowlers develop thick calluses on their thumbs usually at the root of the thumb, and the hardened skin sometimes splits. This can be very painful and needs to be protected by applying cotton batting and collodion which form a seal over the crack. Mark Roth's thumb cracks so badly at times he has to take several weeks off to allow it to heal.

Mark Roth

cranker

n: a bowler who cranks, that is, lifts and turns the ball high over his head

Bob Handley

on his backswing to get extreme speed on his ball. Crankers are notoriously wild bowlers.

creeper

n: a slow ball.

crooked arm

n: a hook ball bowler who bends his elbow.

crow hopper

n: loose, clawlike grip on the ball at release point.

curtain

n: anchor man missing in the final frame when a spare would have won for his team.

Don Carter

curve

n: a ball that breaks from right to left in a huge arc for a righthander; left to right for a lefthander.

cutter

n: a sharp-breaking hook which seems to slice the pins down.

Darts

n: the distinctive marks inserted in the surface of the lanes to give bowlers aiming points. According to ABC regulations darts must be positioned between

(darts cont'd)

12 and 16 feet beyond the foul-line. Each dart must be no more than 1¼" in width, 6" in length, and equidistant from each other.

dead apple

n: an ineffective ball that fades or deflects badly when it hits the pins. Also called a dead ball.

dead wood

n: downed pins that remain on the lane after a hit are called dead wood. They must be removed before the next shot is taken.

deflection

n: the physical reaction of the ball as it strikes the pins and then angles away to one side or the other.

dime store

n: the 5~10 split. Also called a Woolworth.

dive

vt: the action of a ball that hooks greatly at the last split second.

D.O.A.

n: "dead on arrival." A ball with no action or power as it hits the pocket. Such a ball often results in a split.

dodo ball

n: an illegally weighted bowl~ing ball. Sometimes extra weight is put into the hitting side (the left for a righthanded bowler). The result is more power delivered to the pins at impact. The action of a dodo ball can be likened to that of the errat~ic wobbling action of a dying top.

double

n: two strikes in a row. This gives the bowler a score of twenty plus the total pins knocked down with his next ball.

double pinochle

n: the 4~6~7~10 split, same as "big ears," "big four."

Marshall Holman

double wood

n: any two pins, when one is directly behind the other, the 1~5, 2~8 and 3~9.

dovetails

n: the area of the lane where the maple and pine boards join. Also called splice, piano keys, break of the boards.

dump the ball

v: the act of throwing the ball with an unbent stiff sliding knee. The result is a ball that clunks

(dump the ball cont'd)

down on the lane from a height of a foot or more. Lane operators hate bowlers who dump the ball because they cause pock~ marks on the surface of the lane.

Dutch 200

n: a score resulting from al~ ternating spares and strikes with a score of twenty in every frame. A Dutch 200 can begin either with a strike or spare in the first frame.

Emblem

n: the logo on a bowling ball, usually signifying the heaviest part of the ball.

error

n: failure to knock down all the pins in two attempts. Also called an open frame, a miss, or a blow.

Faith, hope, charity

n: the 2~7~10 or 3~7~10 split, the same as Christmas tree.

fast

n: in different sections of the country the mean~ ing is exactly the opposite. In one area it means a lane that allows a ball to hook easily, while in another area it means a lane that holds down the hook.

field goal

n: a ball rolled between two pins of a wide split.

fill

n: pins knocked down in the next frame after a spare.

finger grips

n: there are many different types of finger grips inserted in the finger holes or fastened to the fingers. They are used to help the bowler not only hang onto the ball, but also help him impart spin at delivery. A rubber or plastic insert is often used as is old fashioned adhesive tape.

fingertip

n: a type of finger hole drilled so that only the fingertips of the third and fourth fingers can be inserted in the ball. Because of the wide span even greater than usual spin can be imparted. It requires a very strong wrist to hold and deliver the ball properly and takes a great deal of practice to master.

Don Johnson

flat ball

n: an ineffective ball with few revolutions and little action.

floater

n: a ball that goes where the lane lets it. A ball released badly with no

(floater cont'd)
particular lift or turn.

foul line

n: the line at the front of a bowling alley sixty feet from the center of the number one pin spot. A player must not step or slide across or touch this line when delivering the ball. If he does he commits a foul and scores zero pins on that roll.

foundation

n: a ninth frame strike lays the foundation or the base for a possible three more strikes in the tenth frame.

foundation, early

n: a strike in the eighth frame.

four-bagger

n: four strikes in a row. Five would be a five-bagger. The bowler is said to be stringing strikes.

Wayne Webb

four-step line

n: markers set into the surface of the lane near the rear of the approach. Most four- and five-step bowlers start from the four-step line. They adjust the length of their strides and slide so that they end up with the sliding foot a few inches behind the foul line.

frame

n: a game of bowling has ten frames. In each of the ten frames the bowler attempts to knock down all ten pins on the first roll or failing that on his second.

frozen rope

n: a ball rolled with excessive speed almost straight into the pocket.

Mark Baker

fudge

vt: to decrease the revolutions on the ball. Also to kill the ball by not putting usual lift on it at delivery.

full hit

n: a ball striking near the center of the headpin on a strike attempt or the middle of any pin you may be aiming at.

full roller

n: a bowler's ball that rolls down the lane on a track exactly around its circumference, much like the equator line around the middle of the earth. The consistent tracking of the ball on the same place every roll causes a distinctive wear spot on the ball. If there is no regular track it shows that the bowler is

(full roller cont'd)

not rolling the ball the same way every time, an unde~ sirable fault.

Garbage hit

n: a hit that doesn't enter the pocket but results in a strike anyway because of the mixing action of the pins.

getting the wood

vt: to get a better than average score. Also mak~ ing sure you take one or more pins down on an al~ most impossible split.

grab

vt: to cause a sudden hook because the friction between the lane and the ball is good.

grandma's teeth

n: a random array of pins left standing.

grasshopper

n: an effective ball, particu~ larly on light pocket hits.

graveyards

n: low scoring lanes. In a high~ scoring center it applies to the hardest scoring lanes in the house.

groove

Presidential bowlers:
Harry Truman

n: ball track or indentation in lane. Also a bowler who is performing well and has his approach and arm~swing almost mechanically perfect.

Richard Nixon

gutter

n: the original name for the channel 9 inches wide and 3½ inches deep which runs alongside the lane on both sides. If the ball leaves the lane and drops into the gutter it is out of play. Sometimes a ball will go into the gutter and then ricochet back onto the lane and knock down a pin or two. If it does, those extra pins do not count.

gutter ball

n: a ball that drops off the surface of the lane and into the gutter or channel. It causes a zero score for that ball.

gutter shot

Gutter shot expert
Billy Hardwick

n: a style of delivery in which the bowler rolls his ball from the extreme right or left edge of the lane almost dropping it into the gutter or channel as it goes out over the foul line. It is a dangerous

(gutter shot cont'd)
shot because the margin for error is small.

Handicap

n: pins awarded to individuals or teams in an attempt to equalize competition.

high board

n: a board in a lane may expand or contract a tiny bit due to atmospheric conditions, but enough to change the course of a bowling ball. Most boards contract leaving a low area or a low board, but it is still mis~termed a high board.

high hit

n: a ball that contacted a pin near its center, es~pecially such a hit on the head pin.

holding alley

n: a lane that resists hook action of a ball.

home alley

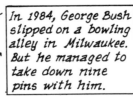

In 1984, George Bush slipped on a bowling alley in Milwaukee. But he managed to take down nine pins with him.

n: favorite lane or pair of lanes for individuals or teams.

hook

n: a ball that breaks sharply to the left (righthander) or right (lefthander).

hook alley

n: a lane on which the ball will move to the left easily.

In there

prep. phrase: a good pocket hit.

Jam

vt: force the ball high into the pocket.

Jersey side

n: to the left of the headpin. Also Brooklyn side.

Kegler

n: a bowler. It comes from the German word kegeln, meaning, to bowl.

kickback

n: side partitions at the end of the lane made of hard vulcanized fiber. They are meant to protect the sides of the lane from the heavy abuse of pins hitting them constantly and also to ensure consistent action off the sideboards from lane to lane all over the country. Sometimes a pin will kick back and take out the second pin of an "impossible" split.

kill the ball

v: take off the spin or action on the ball by not

(Kill the ball cont'd)

lifting or spinning it at the delivery point. This causes the ball to curve less and because it runs straighter the bowler can be more accurate on such difficult spares as the 10~pin or 6~10 pins.

kindling wood

n: light pins.

kingpin

n: the 5~pin in the center of the ten pins is called the kingpin because it must be knocked down in order for a strike to occur. Its action is very important in taking out other pins. The bowling ball only strikes a few of the ten pins so the bowler must rely on pin action to knock down the rest.

kitty

n: money collected from team members for misses, low games, and other set fines. Used to defray expenses in tour~ naments or divided equally at end of season.

Lane

n: the bowling alley, a wooden deck 62~ feet 10¾~ inches long and 42~inches wide. The lane begins with a foul line which is exactly 60 feet from the center of the 1~pin or headpin in a setup of ten pins in a triangle with each pin spaced 12 inches away from the next one.

Aleta Sill

late 10

n: when the 10~pin hesitates, and is the last to go down on a strike.

leadoff man

n: the first bowler, the spark plug of a league team. He is chosen because he is a consistent marker and can get the team off to a good start.

leave

n: those pins not knocked down by the first ball. For example: "He left a 10~pin" or "His leave was a 3~10 split."

leverage

n: the power or lift that a bowler in good position at the line is able to impart to the ball. Sliding to the line with bent knee, hand on the side of the ball or directly behind it, a good bowler has tremendous leverage on the ball as he lifts it or spins it on its way down the lane.

Earl Anthony

lift

n: the upward motion of the ball imparted by the fingers at the moment of release.

light

n: not full on the target headpin, but just touching it.

light wood

n: bowling pins that weigh between three pounds and three pounds~two ounces are called light wood. Three~pound~six~ounce wood is required for ABC competition but bowling proprietors often use light wood in open bowling to help the average bowler knock down more pins—and to get the bowlers to complete games more quickly.

lily

n: the 5~7~10 split.

line

n: another name for a single game of bowling. Also the track the bowler chooses on the lane to give himself the best chance to make a strike.

line ball

n: a straight ball or one with very little hook is called a line ball. It is usually thrown at great speed which causes it to hold the line and snap into the pocket at the very end. It can be a very effective ball because it does not cross as many boards as a curve ball which goes out and then back to the pins.

Mike Aulby

loafing

part: not lifting or turning

the ball properly, with the result that the ball lags and doesn't reach the target, usually rolling off to the right.

loft the ball

v: to deliver the ball on the fly out over the lane a distance which can vary from a few inches to as much as two to three feet. Loft is often used on sticky lanes to cut down on the run of the ball and hold it in the pocket.

logs

n: very heavy wood pins up to four pounds in weight. Good bowlers use them in practice because they know that if they can knock down logs, they can knock down anything lighter.

looper

n: an extra~wide hook ball, usually slow.

lose count

v: to miss pins that could have been knocked down. For example: After a strike in the previous frame, a bowler leaves the 6~7~10 split. If he makes the 6~10 on his second ball he scores 19+9=28. If he gets only the 6~pin he gets 18+8=26, so he loses count— two pins.

love tap

n: a delicate stroke with the powering pin coming

(love tap)

back off the side wall, as if an after~ thought, stroking the neck of the standing pin and causing it to fall.

Makeable split

Andy Varipapa

n: a split that can be converted because one or more of the pins are on a line forward of the others. For ex~ ample: baby splits, the 3~10 and the 3~9, should be made 4 out of 5 times by a good bowler. A split like the 6~7~10 or 5~7 requires more skill on the bowler's part to strike the front pin so precisely that it is driven across the lane into the other pin so as to take it out.

mark

n: a spare, a conversion, a closed frame. A bowler who does not strike on his first ball has a leave of any number of pins. If he knocks down the re~ maining pins with his second ball he is said to mark.

match play

n: a tournament in which teams or individuals are bowling against each other, head to head instead of against the field. The winner is the bowler or team of bowlers that piles up the greatest total of victories.

messenger

n: a pin that comes rolling across the lane out of nowhere and takes out the 10~pin.

miss

n: a failure to knock down all the pins in two attempts to do so. Also called a blow, an error, or an open.

Mister Average

n: the name given to the absent bowler whose average is taken in his place. Usually ten pins are knocked off his score. In a womens' league, of course, it is Mrs. Average who is missing.

mixer

n: a ball with action causing the pins to bounce around.

mother~in~law

n: a sleeper pin, one that hides behind another and thus is less readily seen. It is usually a tandem set~up with the mother~in~law directly behind the front pin as in the 2~8 leave. Another famous mother~in~law occurs in the 2~4~5~8 spare leave in which the 8~pin is the mother~in~law. It is one of the most difficult spares a bowler faces.

move in

vt: to start from or near center of approach.

move out

vt: to start from or near corner position on ap~proach.

One in the dark

n: rear pin in the 1~5, 2~8 or 3~9 spare.

on the nose

prep. phrase: a head~on hit right into the 1~pin. This frequently causes a split.

open

n: a frame in which the bowler did not get a strike or a spare.

out and in

n: a wide hook rolled from the center of the lane toward the gutter. The ball hooks back to the pocket—going out, then in.

over

n: the number of pins above the 200 average is the number of pins over. A 200 average is used as par in professional bowling scoring.

overturn the ball

Amleto Monacelli

v: to put too much spin and not enough lift on the ball at the deliv~ery point. The thumb should come out first to allow the fingers to lift the ball forward and spin it to the side. When the thumb stays in too long, the ball is said to be overturned. It's a bad fault that kills the ball, that is, prevents it from having proper action.

Part of the building

n: a 10~pin standing un~ touched after a smashing strike hit is said to be part of the building, unmoved, unmoveable. Also known as part of the house.

PBA

n: The Professional Bowlers Association, the group of today's professional bowlers that sets the conditions for members (a 200 average is one) and determines the en~ try fee(s) for local and national tournaments. It is the watchdog of professional bowlers and monitors conduct for unprofessional behavior.

perfect game

n: twelve strikes in a row with a count of 30 pins per frame resulting in a 300 game.

Jeanne Maiden

picket fence

n: the 1~2~4~7 or 1~3~6~10 spares.

pie alleys

n: lanes that are easy to bowl on. Scores are generally higher here than elsewhere. Lane operators sometimes "fix" lanes so there is a track right into the 1~3 pocket so that the average bowler can strike more often.

pin bowling

n: the use of the entire pin set~up as a target in~ stead of focusing on a line or spot on the lane. Now that we have the dart or arrow system of lane marking, very few bowlers are pin bowlers. At one time when the splice of the boards had wooden keys that were all the same color, it was difficult to pick out a particular board for a target. Bowl~ ers then had to pin bowl out of necessity.

pinch the ball

vt: to grip the ball too hard.

pindicator

n: the lighted display board behind the lane which shows the bowler what pins he has knocked down and which pins remain to be knocked down.

pine

n: softer wood used beyond divi~ sion boards, takes over where maple ends.

George Pappas

pit

n: the area beyond the pin deck into which the pins and balls fall.

pitch

n: the angle at which a finger hole is drilled into a bowling ball. Reverse pitch is a drilling that heads backward away from the front of the ball. Positive pitch is the

(pitch cont'd)

opposite. You must trust your neighbor-hood balldriller to drill the proper pitch that fits your hand and deli-very.

plugged ball

n: a ball that does not fit the bowler's hand can be easily re-drilled with new fingerholes. A plastic mate-rial called a plug is used to fill the old holes. A plugged ball works just as well as an unplugged ball in most instances.

Loa Boxberger

pocket

n: the area between the 1- and 3-pins for the righthanded bowler. It is the 1 and 2 for the left-hander. The ball must enter the pocket and have enough power to reach the 5-pin which is the kingpin in the heart of the pin set-up.

point the ball

v: to attempt to get into the pocket by aiming it higher on the headpin. It is a risky move because one inch too much and you have snake-eyes, a wide open split.

poison ivy

n: the troublesome 3-6-10 split.

poodle

vt: to roll a gutter ball.

powder puff

n: a slow ball that fails to carry the pins. Also, a puff ball.

powerhouse

n: an extremely strong first ball, one that rips up the pins even when it just ticks the headpin. Usually, it is rolled with good speed and puts all ten pins into the pit, sweeping the deck.

puddle

n: a gutter ball.

pull the rug

v: to have the ball just touch the headpin and make all the pins start to dance. They move around, standing up, until the last second when they all seem to collapse at once resulting in a strike. That's when it is said that the bowler pulls the rug.

pumpkin

n: another one of the many colorful names for an ineffective ball. It is one without the necessary spin that produces action at the pocket.

Quick eight

n: a good pocket hit which leaves the 4~7 for righthanders, 6~10 for lefthanders.

Railroad

n: a wide open split with both pins on the same line. Examples, the 4~6, the 7~9 and the 8~10.

range finders

n: two sets of markers embedded in the surface of the lane. One is a set of ten dots seven feet beyond the foul line. The other is nine feet farther down the lane in a triangular arrangement of seven arrows. Both are used to help the bowler establish a target line to the pocket.

rat club

n: a team that shoots horribly low scores for one game.

reading the lanes

vt: discovering whether a lane hooks or holds, and where the best place is to roll the ball to score high.

Dick Weber

release

n: the moment of truth in the bowling delivery when the arm and hand pass the sliding foot at the fraction of a second when the bowler "hits the line" and the ball is lofted out a few inches over the foul line.

reset

n: a bowler is allowed to call for a re~ setting of the pins when pins are set down on the lane "offspot" by the pinsetter, that is, not precisely where they should be. Pre~ viously when pin boys set the pins it was not unheard of for a bowler to bribe the pinsetter to set the 5~pin offspot. By doing that he could almost guarantee that his opponent would draw an 8~10 split.

reverse

n: a ball that backs up, that is, moves in the opposite direction from which it was intended.

Mike Durbin

revolutions

n: the turns a ball takes to go from the foul line to the pins.

ringing 10~burner

n: a crashing strike right into the pocket will some~ times get only nine pins down. When the 10~pin stands, it is said that the strike ball was a ringing 10~burner. The bowler is also said to be tapped.

rotation

Mark Roth

n: the spin imparted to the ball at the moment of delivery. The more spin, the more pin action. Powerful bowler Mark Roth gets more rotation or turns than a weaker bowler. That is why he gets more pins.

rug jerker

n: a 5~pin that is swept out to the right on a strike ball as if someone had jerked a rug out from under it.

Sandbagger

n: a bowler who intentionally throws away a spare when his team is either a certain winner or loser without his score. He may lower his true average by 8 to 10 pins and thus have an unfair advantage in bowling against others when averages are used to determine the winners. A team of five sandbaggers theo~ retically can lower their true averages by as much as 50 pins. In a tournament with total averages restricted to 850 it is obvious that the sandbaggers increase their chances to win.

scenic route

n: path taken by big curve ball.

schleifer

n: a thin hit strike where pins seem to fall one by one.

scratch

n: rolling without benefit of handicap. The actual score.

semi~fingertip

n: a ball~drilling that causes the ball to rest on the pads between the second and

(semi~fingertip cont'd)

third joints of the third and fourth fingers. More power~ful than a conventional grip, less powerful than a full fingertip, it requires strong wrists to make it work well.

semi~roller

n: a ball that rolls on a track just outside the thumb~hole. It is also called a semi~spinner. Probably the most powerful style of delivery, it is the one that produces the most strikes and the most power at the pocket.

shadow ball

n: a ball rolled in practice without the pins being set. It is frequently used in bowling tournaments with each bowler being allowed one shadow ball on each lane before starting.

short pin

n: a pin rolling on the alley that doesn't reach and hit a standing pin.

shotgun shot

n: rolling the ball from the hip.

sidewheeling

n: the act of allowing the arm with the ball to wrap around the body in the backswing. A very bad fault, it re~sults in a ball with little or no action.

slot

n: a depression in the lane worn into a

track by ball after ball taking the same path. A ball rolled in the slot almost automatically comes up into the pocket. Easy lanes with lots of slots are known as slot alleys or pie alleys from the expression easy as pie.

slot grip

n: a grip on the bowling ball with the area between the third and fourth fingers drilled away so, in effect, there are not two fingerholes but one big one with both third and fourth fingers using it.

small ball

n: a ball that doesn't mix the pins. It must hit the pocket perfectly to get a strike. It seems smaller but isn't.

snake-eyes

n: a wide-open split with pins on the same line, the 7-10.

Tommy Hudson

snow plow

n: a ball that clears all the pins for a strike.

soft lanes

n: lanes that are easy to score on. Also called slot alleys.

sour apple

n: a bowling ball that is dead, without action, without

(sour apple cont'd)
stuff on the ball. Also known as a pumpkin
because of the hollow, weak sound it
makes as it hits the pins.

Bob
Strampe

span

n: the distance on a bowling ball between
the thumb and the other fingerholes.

spare

n: if all ten pins are not knocked
down on the first ball of a frame and
the second ball knocks down the rest, the bowler
has a spare.

splasher

n: a strike where the pins are downed quickly.

splice

n: the area in the lane where the pine boards and
the maple are fitted together. It is 20 feet down from the
foul line. In the early days of bowling dark and light
boards at that location gave the bowlers a target for
aiming. With the addition of the arrows or darts embedded in the surface of the lane, bowlers in modern
days have much more accurate target systems.

split

n: a spare leave in which the headpin is down and the
remaining combination of pins have an intermediate pin
down immediately ahead of or between them.

spot bowling

n: bowling by aiming at a spot on the lane rather than at the pins themselves. In line bowling the bowler envisions a line to the pocket in which he wants his ball to travel. In spot bowl~ ing the bowler often will adjust his spot to the left or right depending upon whether his ball is hitting the pocket high or low.

Marion Ladewig

squeeze

n: the action of the second and third fingers against the thumb, much like snapping the fingers, as they de~ liver the bowling ball out over the foul line.

steal

vt: to get more pins than you deserve on a strike hit.

stiff lanes

n: lanes on which the ball does not curve very much—contrasted with run~ ning lanes on which the ball does curve.

strike

n: knocking down all ten pins on the first ball rolled.

strike out

v: to get all three strikes in the tenth frame. Originally bowlers

Sylvia Wene Martin

(strike out cont'd)

Teata Semiz

rolled three times in each frame. Then, in the early 1900s the scoring was changed to two balls per frame with a scoring bonus of 10 pins if all the pins were knocked down on either the first attempt or the first two attempts. The third ball in the 10th frame is a holdover from old time bowling.

strike split

n: the 8~10 split in the back row, so called because the leave occurs on what apparently is a good strike ball in the pocket.

string

n: three or more strikes in a row constitute a string of strikes.

stroke

n: the act of delivery, the arm and hand motion as the ball is delivered over the foul line. Earl Anthony has a smooth, consistent stroke. Mark Roth does not stroke the ball but throws it.

Swiss cheese ball

n: a hole~filled ball used to determine a bowler's finger size and span so a ball can be drilled to fit the bowl~er's hand exactly.

Take off a mark

vt: reduce the running score of marks by one. In team bowling it is customary to total the number of marks per frame as each team progresses. Either a spare or strike counts as one mark. A triple, three strikes in a row, is counted as two doubles. A double, two strikes in a row, counts as two. For example, if a 5~man team bowls 4 spares and a miss in one frame it has 4 marks in that frame. A team bowling 3 spares and 2 doubles would have 7 marks. A mark anticipates a good count of 7 or more pins. When a bowler has a short count of 5 pins or less on a spare or double, the call is to take off a mark. Note — it is always the *other* team that makes the call with great glee.

tap

n: a stubborn 10~pin, 4~pin, or an 8~pin that refuses to fall on what appears to be a solid strike hit.

Charlie Tapp

team captain

n: in league bowling, every team has a captain who is held responsible for all the members showing up to bowl. He arranges for a substitute bowler or bowlers when others are absent or ill. He is also the team strategist who determines bowling lineup with a strong leadoff man and a strong anchorman.

telephone poles

n: heavy pins. Also logs.

"the fire's out"

n: a common expression from the opponents when a string of strikes comes to an end.

thin hit

n: a ball that goes into the pocket and barely touches the headpin. If it causes a strike, it drives the opponents mad because the ball really does not look strong enough to do so. Don Carter was the master of the thin hit, grazing the headpin so slightly that often it fell forward toward the left.

Don Carter

300 game jinx

n: when a bowler starts a game with a string of strikes there is always the possibility that he will roll twelve in a row and score a 300 game. The belief is that no one should mention such a possibility because if anyone does the string is sure to be broken.

Another custom concerning a 300 game is that when a bowler has rolled nine strikes in a row, the rest of the league all will stop bowling and allow the 300 game candidate to bowl his tenth frame all alone. An unusual event occurred in 1957 when Reno Ministrelli and George Young were each bowling in the third man slots against each other. Each man had nine strikes in a row. Reno stepped up and rolled three more for his 300 game. The bowlers in the gallery went wild. Then George Young stepped up on the adjacent lane and did the same thing. It was one of the rare occasions when side by side 300 games were rolled.

three-quarters

n: the spot where bowlers place the ball upon delivery midway between right corner and center of lane and three-fourths of the width of the lane from the left corner. A popular starting point.

three-step line

n: the area twelve feet from the foul line marked by dowels. It is often used as the starting position by a three-step bowler.

throwing rocks

vt: piling up strikes with a speed ball.

Mark Roth

tickler

n: when the 6-pin comes off the right hand side board and strokes the 10-pin in a gentle manner it is said to tickle the 10-pin so the 6-pin is the tickler. Don Carter was a famous practitioner of the tickler shot. His strike ball always seemed to leave the 10-pin standing and then, as if on command, the 6-pin would tickle the 10-pin and stroke it down.

top the ball

v: when a bowler keeps his thumb in the ball too long at delivery he is said to top the ball. The necessary fingerlift is missing and the ball will have no power or action at the pins. Also called thumbing the ball.

tumbler

n: a strike in which the pins are not smashed into the pit but appear to fall individually. Sometimes the pinfall of a tumbler is achieved slowly with a couple of pins standing until the last second and then falling.

Earl Anthony

turkey

n: three strikes in a row. Also called a triple.

turn

vt: motion of hand and wrist toward pocket area at point of ball release.

Umbrella ball

n: a high hit on the nose resulting in a strike.

under

n: the number of pins below the 200 average that is considered par in professional bowling scoring.

Venting

vt: drilling a small hole (not a finger hole) to relieve suction in the thumb hole.

Washout

n: the 1~2~10 leave which results when the ball

cuts in behind the headpin on a first ball. Not a split because the headpin is still standing. Can be made by striking the 1~2 combination so as to throw the headpin over into the 10 and take it out. The 1~2~4~10 is called a washout.

water in the ball

n: a weak ball that results in an 8~10, 5~7, or 5~10 leave.

wood

n: in handicapping, the number of pins given ("How much wood will you give me?"), or in scoring, the number of pins knocked down ("He got all the wood.").

working ball

n: a ball with enough action to mix the pins on an offpocket hit and scramble them for a strike.

wrap around

n: on an apparently good strike ball sometimes the 6~pin bounces off the side board and misses the 10~pin leaving it standing. The 6~pin action is called a wrap~ around because that's what it looks like.

wrist master

n: one of many contraptions made of vinyl, leather, steel, or similar material and strapped to the bowler's wrist and hand to help him keep a firm wrist through

(wrist master cont'd)
his backswing and delivery.

wrist turn

n: the turning action of the wrist at the moment
of ball release. The ball can be delivered with or
without wrist turn. Each style has its advantages.

X

n: in scoring, the symbol for strike.

Yank the shot

vt: when a bowler hangs on to the ball too long
and pulls it across his body.

Zero in

*Glenn
Allison*

vt: find the right strike spot or
line on a lane.

NICKNAMES

Glenn (900) Allison

He rolled three successive 300 games recently to break the long-standing three game record, 300-300-278, set in 1937 by Allie Brandt. Then poor Glenn found that the American Bowling Congress would not recognize his score as official because the lanes he bowled on were not up to ABC standards.

Mark (Moon) Baker

Tall, 6-feet-4, he's the PBA champion bowler who gained national attention when the seat of his pants split and revealed that he was wearing no underwear. Also called "Moon Over Miami" because that's where the event occurred.

Ray (The Photographer) Bluth

He looks like an old-fashioned photographer when he takes aim on the pins, peering over his ball held close in front of his eyes, making tiny delicate adjustments to the right or left, up or down, before he finally rolls the ball.

Nelson (Bo) Burton, Jr.

His younger brothers could not pronounce his fam~ily nickname of "Brother." Bo was easier. He has one of the greatest records in ABC history and is a crack sports announcer.

Lou (Wrong Foot) Campi

Star bowler of the 1930s and 1940s, he approached the foul line with a right foot slide rather than the con~ventional left. His stop was abrupt but the action he put on the ball was terrific. An early television bowling star, he won fifteen head to head matches in a row.

Don (Bosco) Carter

He claims he was puny as a child and was raised on the children's malted drink, Bosco — therefore the nickname.

Grazio (Graz) Castellano

One of the early stars of televised bowling in the East, he had a powerful hook that murdered the pins and his oppo~nents.

Johnny (The General) Crimmins

Because he was a take~charge Captain of the champion Stroh bowling team, he was nicknamed "The General." Crimmins was a noted needler of his opponents. All he had to do was ask, "You've changed your delivery since I last saw you, haven't you?" and the opponent would blow up. He was named Bowler of the Year in 1942, the first time the title was awarded.

Joe (Chesty) Falcaro

His spindly legs and normal body were topped by a monstrous chest that gave him his nickname. A powerful hook bowler and a great anchorman, he could produce 10th frame strikes when his team needed them.

Basil Ignazio (Buzz) Fazio

The name Buzz evolved from his name Basil. Also Known as "Bee-Eye" from his initials. Buzz was famous for his enthusiasm, which often found him on his knees two lanes away after a crucial strike.

Don (Big Foot) Genalo

He was given this nickname because he is reported to have the biggest feet on the Professional Bowling Tour.

Harry (Goose) Golden

He got this nickname because as tour director of the Professional Bowlers Tour he's the "goose that laid the golden egg." A former Pro bowler himself, he has supervised more than 800 successive tournaments without missing one. He is so popular he was named to the Bowlers Hall of Fame in 1984.

Billy (Billy G) Golembiewski

G is easier to pronounce than Golembiewski. A slight fellow who rolled a straight ball with unerring accuracy, he was one of the few successful bowlers with that style.

Jeff (The Great White Whale) Mattingly

Physical appearance is a fertile field for nick~names. Mattingly is a big, heavy man, topped with a shock of pure white hair so comparison with a whale followed easily.

James (Junie) McMahon

He came by this nickname naturally, distinguishing him from his father who was a great bowler of the 1890s and early 1900s. He used a specially drilled ball, which he kept secret from his opponents for

(Junie McMahon cont'd)

years. Even when they discovered how he did it, his oppo~
nents still could not roll the ball as well as Junie did.

Walter (Skang) Mercurio

He was married to Stella Skankowski who came to the
lanes regularly to cheer him on. His opponents would
rag him by saying, "Hey, Walter, Skang's here!" The nick~
name stuck to him. He was one of the best bowlers of
the 1930s.

Carmen (Spook) Salvino

He is called Spook because he has
Bela Lugosi eyes and therefore, looks
spooky. He is a great student of the
physics and mechanics of the strike
ball. At the age of 53, ancient by
modern day standards, he is a
wonder bowler who has won
seventeen PBA tournaments.

Ernie (U.S.A.) Schlegel

Because he wears bright
sequin~decorated outfits in
the colors, red, white, and
blue, the colors of the flag,
Schlegel was given this obvious
nickname.

Curt (The Martian) Schmidt

According to the other
bowlers on the tour, Schmidt

(Curt Schmidt cont'd)
seems to be in outer space a good bit of the time. Ergo, The Martian.

Dave (Soupy) Soutar

A tall, languorous, star bowler whose approach is unusually slow and deliberate, Soupy followed easily from his bowling style and his name.

Tony (Mr. Headpin) Sparando

One of the best bowlers of the late 1930s and early 1940s in the New Jersey~New York area, he is said to have gone three complete seasons without missing the headpin. And they say he never crossed over, either!

John (Guppy) Troup

He is called that because his mouth works like a guppy's and also because he raises tropical fish. He once complained that he had lost an impor~ tant bowling match because he had been up all night with a sick guppy.

Walter (The Cigar) Ward

This famous Cleveland All~Star bowler of the 1940s and 1950s always bowled with an unlighted crooked stogie in his mouth. He was famous for keeping records of every game he ever bowled. He had more 700 series than anyone else in bowling history.

Joe (Buck) Wilman

Well~known for his deep pockets when it came to paying a check, he would reach down and say, "I've got a buck here" and before he produced it, someone else would pay the check for him. A great bowler in the Chicago area in the 1940s and early 1950s.

CHRIS SCHENKEL

Chris Schenkel is one of the best known sports announcers in the radio and television business. He is one of the finest stylists in his field, possessing a smooth, unexcitable voice that conveys expert knowledge about many different sports. He never hesitates in his speech, never uses cliché fillers, and, all in all, conveys to the listener a sense of professional dignity.

Chris Schenkel took his first job in 1942 as a radio sportscaster in Muncie, Indiana. The pay was $18 a week. Chris decided early in his career that he wanted to cover a wide spectrum of sports rather than specialize in just one or two. Based on what he has accomplished in 35 straight years as a network announcer, he has no reason to regret that decision.

The ABC sportscaster has covered virtually every major sports event in his long, successful career. His most recent honor came when he was elected to the National Sportscasters and Sports Writers Association Hall of Fame in 1981. Before that he had been named Sportscaster of the Year by the same group of his peers in 1963, 1964, 1967 and 1970.

Chris was one of the first to report football on national television. He began with the Harvard games in 1947 and since then he has covered more than 500 professional and college football games for television. For 13 years he was the voice of the New York Giants and also reported National Football League games for CBS.

He has covered more boxing matches on television than any other sportscaster, having called the Monday Night Fights, five or six bouts a night, for six straight years, 50 weeks a year, beginning in 1953.

And then bowling became a part of his life. The PBA, founded in 1958 with 33 charter members, held its first tournaments in 1959. Then in 1960 came the first televised program, *Make That Spare.* In 1962 *The Pro Bowlers Tour* hit Saturday afternoon television screens in America with Chris Schenkel as the announcer, a role he has filled ever since. Today the series is ABC's longest running sports show, and it seems it will be for some time to come.

Chris said that the funniest thing he ever saw on the bowling program occurred the night Mark Baker's pants split revealing the fact that he was wearing no underwear. "That was an eye-opening experience," he said, and laughed as he commented that he believed it wouldn't happen again since the other bowlers deluged Baker with presents of new underwear after the happening. He said, "Baker is now known as 'Moon Baker.' "

Chris has had wide experience in all sports broadcasting, but it is his career as a bowling announcer that has brought him his greatest fame and perhaps his most personal satisfaction. Chris is so well regarded by the professional bowlers of America that in 1976 he was named a member of the Professional Bowlers Hall of Fame, recognition of the importance of his role in broadcasting the sport and making it popular throughout the country.

One of the biggest oddities in Chris' TV bowling career concerns the fact that in the long history of the program, *Pro Bowlers Tour,* some 1500 games have been bowled, but only three times have there been 300 games rolled "on camera." Not one of them did Chris see. For one reason or another, he was absent on those occasions.

A probable surprise to many sports fans is the fact that Chris is also a movie actor and has had roles in five feature films, *Requiem for a Heavyweight, Goodbye Columbus, Maurie, Dreamer,* and *International Velvet.* Chris said that one of the thrills of his life was to be involved with Anthony Quinn in the making of *Requiem for a Heavyweight.* He said that the physical presence of Quinn is almost overpowering and that Quinn is in remarkable shape for a man of his age. The *Dreamer* part was a natural one for him since the film dealt with a bowler who dreamed of becoming a champion.

Chris has also been the "Voice" of the Masters for many years. He has a great love for the golf tournament, which he claims is the "finest in the world." His big thrill at the Masters came in 1986 when Jack Nicklaus hugged his son, Jackie, on the 18th green after winning at age 46.

Chris is very interested in Indian culture and Indian art. He has an

excellent collection in his home on Lake Tippecanoe in Leesburg, Indiana. Chris is an Honorary Chieftain on the Miami Indian Council of Indiana. When he is carrying out his broadcasting duties, Chris commutes from his cottage home and then returns as fast as he can to his family, two sons, a daughter, and his wife, the former Fran Paige, who was once a June Taylor dancer and a top fashion model in New York.

Chris said that he has really enjoyed his years of broadcasting the bowling tournaments on TV and takes special pleasure in having known intimately such great gentlemen of the bowling world as Earl Anthony, Eddie Elias, and Billy Welu.

MARK ROTH

Mark Roth was born in Brooklyn, New York, in 1951 into a family that lived in modest circumstances. His father died when he was a child and he was raised by his mother and an older sister. When he was eleven years old a new bowling center opened a few blocks from his home. He discovered it, bowled a few times, and soon fell in love with the sport. Every day after school he could not wait to go and knock those pins down. At that very young age he learned to throw the ball at the pins as hard as he could and he found that when he did he was successful in getting strikes. As a teenaged bowler he learned how to put action on the ball.

Of course, there was the problem of getting the money to pay for the games. Bowling cost about 50 cents a line in those days so in order to pay for his bowling, young Mark worked as a handyman in the bowling center. He cleaned the floor, the pins, the ash trays, even the toilets, and in that way he earned the money he needed to bowl.

The owner of the bowling lanes liked Mark and was good to him. It is probable that he could see that he had a future star ascending before his eyes. He allowed Mark to bowl at lower prices than usual, and then he taught him how to work and repair the automatic pin-setting machines. Mark still enjoys jumping into the pit when a machine breaks down to set it in working order. He has even done that recently when he was involved in tournament bowling.

One day when Mark was in his late teens he saw a pro bowler win $3,000 in a televised match. Right then he swore that was the way he was going to make his living. He soon discovered amateur tournaments in which he could win money. These were singles competitions usually across 10 pairs of lanes with big cash prizes for those who knocked down the most pins.

Mark said, "You'd think I had discovered a gold mine! I spent most of my weekends bowling."

At last he felt that he was ready to try his skills against the professionals, so he joined the PBA in 1970 at the age of nineteen. For three long years he struggled. He did not come close to breaking even, earning only a little over $1,000 in 1970, and $2,500 in 1971. In 1972 his earnings jumped to $12,000, and he took second place in the Chicago Brunswick World Open. His earnings increased to $19,000, in 1973, and $36,000, in 1974, but he still did not have a single victory on the tour.

Finally, he broke through in 1975 to win the Kansas City King Louie Open and boosted his earnings to $45,000 for that year. Now he was a bowler to watch for sure. He won three titles in 1976 and pocketed $72,000. In 1977 he won four times and went over the $100,000 mark, an exalted rank attained only by the great Earl Anthony before him.

From then on there was no stopping Mark Roth. His earnings have mounted year after year and three times (in 1977, 1979 and 1984) he has been named Bowler of the Year. Mark Roth is now 35 years of age and has recently joined Earl Anthony as a million dollar prize winner of the PBA tour.

Mark is another one of those controversial bowlers, not quite as disliked as Marshall Holman, but treated coolly by the other bowlers who fear his awesome power. Mark actually intimidates his fellow bowlers by rolling what is probably the most powerful hook ball in bowling history. He rolls the ball so hard and spins it so strongly that he can hold his hook until the ball is only two to six feet from the pins. This is in contrast to most bowlers whose hooks start eight to twelve feet from the pins. The result of Roth's delayed action (and he is one of the very few who can accomplish this successfully frame after frame) is that the ball simply explodes at the 1-3 pocket and smashes the pins to the sideboards from which they ricochet to take out any pins that have dared to stand after the first impact.

Mark Roth has a constantly belligerent attitude on the lanes spiced by a tremendous desire to win. He simply hates to lose and lets everyone know it. He said, "I don't consider myself a nasty person, but when I bowl against someone even if it's a friend or my roommate, even my wife or

my mother, they aren't people I know until the game is over. Each one becomes a challenger, an enemy, someone to beat. Once the game is over everything is forgiven until the next time. It may not be the right way to do it for everyone, but it's my way and it seems to be working for me."

Mark is considered a loner in the bowling scene. He admits that he is and says he dearly loves his privacy.

The top bowling writer, Chuck Pezzano, has commented on Mark Roth saying, "Mark's ego or aloofness is more likely bashfulness. He feels uncomfortable in large crowds, or even small crowds. He prefers to sit off in a corner rather than be a life of the party. He is only comfortable with people he knows well."

Roth has always been affected by recurring problems with the thumb on his bowling hand. He grips the ball tightly and twists it violently in his backswing, and then gives it a vicious reverse twist at the explosion-point of his powerful delivery at the foul line. Some bowlers have had problems caused by the way they deliver the ball. It is not unusual for them to develop callouses on their fingers, especially at the tip of the thumb, or in the web between the thumb and first finger because the bowler inserts his hand deep into the ball at the start of his delivery.

Roth's finger problem has been so severe that at times he has had to retire for a few weeks to allow the swollen, cracked sore to heal. Roth was asked what he does about his sore hand. He said, "If my hands hurts from too much bowling, I just soak it. Don Johnson used to stick his thumb in a potato. I tried it, and it felt good. Sometimes I have to lay off for a while." He has tried many different ball drillings that might put less strain on his thumb, but when he finds one that hurts him less, he loses part of the steam and action on his ball.

Despite this problem, Mark Roth has achieved remarkable results. He holds the most titles in one season, collecting eight in 1978; he has the highest tour average in one season, 221.6 in 1979. In 1980 he rolled three 300 games in one tournament, a feat never surpassed by any other bowler. As well, he has reached the elite cast of the TV five finalists in 115 of 366 career tournaments.

While Earl Anthony leads all the professional bowlers in total career earnings of $1,264,621, Mark Roth has won $1,134,192, counting tournaments through mid-1986. It is likely that Roth will surpass Earl's record some time in 1987. Is Mark Roth the greatest bowler since Earl Anthony? The next few years will tell.

MARION LADEWIG

They call her "Queen Marion." That's Marion Ladewig, the greatest woman bowler who ever lived. She was married at 15, a mother at 17, divorced at 22, and from then on she devoted her entire life to bowling. She's 72 now, and still bowls twice a week.

Petite, only 5-feet-4-inches tall, still 130 pounds, Marion today is in almost as great physical shape as she was in the days when she broke all the women's bowling records. She recalled, "I was a softball player when I was in my teens. I bowled my first game in 1937. It was near the end of the softball season and some of the stars of the team took a couple of rookies, like me, to bowl some practice games in the winter season. I remember my first game," she added, "an 84. Before the winter season was over, I had my average up to 149."

Marion says that the biggest thrill of her life came when she won the 1951 All-Star Tournament in head-to-head competition with the best men and women bowlers of that day. The title was her sixth national match game crown. In four sets of two games, she totaled 1981, an average of 247. She rolled an opening pair of games, 225-229-584, an All-Star mark that stands to this day.

Two hours later she rolled a 471 in games of 247-224. Another two hours later she posted 247-227-474 and her final pair were 255-247-502 for the overall 1981. Her average of 211 for the 32 game finals was better than any of the men's including the men's champion, Junie McMahon.

Marion was a member of the Brunswick instructional staff for twenty-nine years from 1950 to 1979. She retired at the age of 65. She traveled extensively in Europe for Brunswick and was a great factor in publicizing the game of bowling overseas. Until she visited many foreign cities, and demonstrated her bowling abilities, the sport was considered one primarily for men. Marion visited Switzerland, Sweden, Germany, France, Belgium, Italy, Australia, and Africa. Today there are millions of women bowlers trying to emulate Marion's smooth style.

Although Marion traveled for years, she said she never did the sightseeing that she would have liked to do. "I was always saving myself for the bowling. I didn't go here or there because if I did, I knew I'd have to sacrifice my bowling. The nice thing about representing Brunswick," Marion said, "is that whenever I won prize money, the company would match it. The biggest purses I won were $5,000 each for the All-Star and the World Invitational. Those were tremendous purses in those days. I saved my money carefully and when the time came I was able to buy a part ownership in the Fanatorium Bowling Lanes in Grand Rapids. That has proved to be one of the smartest moves of my life because it provides me to this day with a substantial income and it keeps me active in the bowling game, which I truly love."

Marion said that her bowling was one of the major causes of her marriage break up in 1940. "I wound up with a job in a bowling center. Naturally, back then, when you worked in a place like that you worked at night. So it was either give up bowling to be with my husband at night or else. I took the 'or else' alternative. I loved the game so much and I started to bowl well, too. I had never had anything like that in my life before."

Marion rolled a line ball, that is, one that goes straight down the lane usually between the second and third arrows. She relied on her accuracy and a final turn of the ball at the pocket to get her strikes and cover her spares.

She had a serious hand problem at one time. Many bowlers do because the weight of the ball is frequently thrown entirely on one particular knuckle, usually on the third finger of the bowling hand. Marion related, "They call it 'bowler's finger.' The knuckle would swell and become so sore I would have to wrap it with tape to bowl. It finally got so bad I had to have surgery on it. Spurs developed on both sides of the joint and I had to have them cut out of both the first and second joints of my middle finger.

"The doctors did wonders for me because I didn't have to tape it after that. The knuckle is still a little oversize, but it never bothers me any

more. The operation was in 1960 and I did a lot of good bowling after
that."

Although Marion is bothered by arthritis in her hips these days, and has gone to a 12-pound ball, down four pounds from the 16-pounder she used to roll so effectively, she started off last season with a high 650 series and averaged 185 for the entire year. She claimed that rolling the 12-pound ball required a different rhythm on her approach—she obviously got used to it.

This queen of bowling won the National All Star six times, was named Woman Bowler of the Year five times, and, paired with Laverne Haverty (later Mrs. Don Carter), won the Women's International Bowling Congress doubles title four times. A bowling ambassador who travelled around the world for her sport, Marion Ladewig's influence on women's bowling will never be equalled.

MARSHALL HOLMAN

Marshall Holman is the bowler who people everywhere love to hate. When he crashes a strike in a match, he stomps his feet, punches the air, spins around and lets out a snarl. When an opponent makes a big shot, particularly a lucky one, Holman will stick his fingers in his ears to drown out the cheers of the crowd. On the whole, 32-year-old Holman qualifies as a summa cum laude graduate of the Nastase-Connors-McEnroe school of petulant childish behavior. He is a hot dog in a sport that is known for its dignified and sportsmanlike champions. Holman is cocky, arrogant, belligerent, and yet, when the scores are all totalled and the championships counted, he is a frontrunner in the bowling world.

Earl Anthony, a champion known always to be a gentleman, said, "Right now Marshall is taking a lot of heat, but the day will come when he'll polish his act and he'll go from arrogance to colorfulness. We need bowlers who will attract the public."

Not only is Holman an attention-grabber—at times he's impossible to overlook, such as the time he bowled against Jeff Mattingly, a tow-headed pro who has recently come onto the bowling scene as a strong competitor. Jeff needed to get three strikes in his tenth frame to beat Holman and take the lead in the tournament into the final day.

Jeff got his first strike. Marshall kicked a chair and sent it rattling across the approach. Jeff was not upset, it appeared, because he proceeded to smash his second tenth frame strike. Holman kicked the ball rack right next to Mattingly. Jeff rolled the third strike. Holman threw a fit—and nearly everything else in sight.

Holman was suspended from PBA competition for ten tournaments after a series of conduct violations, climaxed by an incident where he kicked the foul light on national television. He also once broke a bone in his bowling hand by punching a wall after leaving a 10-pin during the Firestone Tournament of Champions.

Mark Roth, Holman's great competitor said, "Let Marshall do his thing. That's how he gets pumped up. I think he's great, but there are guys on the tour who hate him."

Carmen Salvino, a long-time champion, said, "Athletes can be colorful in various ways. Some bring out warmth, some bring out laughs. Holman brings out the hostility in the fans. That's not all bad. People want to love and people want to hate."

Most of the bowlers who dislike Holman's conduct refuse to speak up, even off the record, preferring to "let sleeping tigers lie," for when he is riled, Marshall seems to bowl his best.

Holman explained his misbehavior this way: "The bowling center is my office. When things aren't going well for me I let loose. I don't think it's healthy to take your troubles back to your room or your family. I just wish everyone could sit down and have a meal with me. They'd find I'm a decent guy. When I leave the lane I leave my game there. I don't take it home."

Marshall Holman has a slight build, only five-feet-six-inches. He is balding on the top of his head and wears a flashy handlebar moustache. His bowling style is extremely unorthodox until the last second of an explosive delivery at the line. Then his hand and body obey all the fundamentals of squareness to the line, and full follow-through with authority. Marshall crouches over at the start of his delivery. He uses every inch of the approach even going so far that half his rear foot hangs over the back edge of the lane. He stoops over, head down, back arched toward the pins. Then with a sudden rush of short quick steps he makes his delivery of an extremely powerful ball. It simply tears up the pins most of the time.

Holman recently won the prestigious Firestone Tournament of Champions for the second time. He now has 20 tournament victories to his credit and is closing in upon the records of Earl Anthony and Mark Roth in money earned and titles won. Winning the Firestone title made Holman the third career millionaire in PBA history along with Earl Anthony and Mark Roth. He also joins Anthony, Roth, Dick Weber, Don Johnson, and Dick Ritget as PBA's 20-time tour champions.

GLENN ALLISON

Glenn Allison, in 1982 at age 52, after winning four ABC championships, five PBA titles, election to the ABC Hall of Fame, and officially retiring from professional bowling, rolled 36 consecutive strikes in three straight 300 games and stepped into the realm of bowling immortality with his perfect 900 series.

That night, July 1, 1982, was Glenn's girlfriend's birthday. As she, Jessie Thompson, sat in the restaurant of La Habra 300 Bowl in California, Glenn stepped up on lanes 13 and 14 to fulfill his promise to her that he would roll a 300 game in honor of her birthday. He was taking part in a three-man team mixed league game. His teammates were Dennis Curley, who rolled 564 that night, and Glada Acocks, who scored 467. Ironically, Glada had seen Glenn roll his first 300 game in open play when he was only 16 years old.

Jessie Thompson was still in the restaurant of the lanes when she heard lots of cheering. Someone came in and told her that Glenn had just shot a 300 game, "for Jessie, as I promised." She rushed out to the lanes and discovered that Glenn had already rolled two strikes in his second game.

When she complained that she hadn't seen him do it, Glenn said, "Well, there's always the chance I'll throw another." Thirty minutes later Allison delivered his twenty-fourth consecutive ball into the pocket and pumped his right arm as the ball crashed into the pins. His teammates congratulated him wildly and this time Jessie was there to give him a big hug. Glenn had rolled two consecutive 300 games.

There are 30 other lanes at La Habra 300 Bowl, but as Glenn began to bowl his third game in the series, no one made a sound until Glenn released his ball. Waitresses were quiet with their trays of beer; bowlers abandoned their games to group around the crowd already gathered at lanes 13 and 14. Each time Glenn launched another ball the quiet was shattered by exhilarated cheers from the crowd as the ball reached the pins.

Glenn rolled strike number five, strike number six, strike number seven. When the pins all fell down in the eighth frame, Glenn twisted through the massed group of spectators, for everyone in the lanes had gathered to watch Glenn bowl his final frames. He found his brother Bob and confessed, "I'm nervous. My knees are shaking." No wonder. Allison was on the brink of bowling the highest competitive series in bowling history. Four more strikes and he would eclipse Allie Brandt's record of 886 shot in 1939. Allison returned to the lane.

He kept his delivery smooth and his rhythm under control and smashed down the pins for his ninth strike. When he released his ball in the tenth frame, however, Glenn knew he had "pulled it," (let it ride high into the headpin). He knew the ball was too high for a strike as it travelled those sixty feet toward the pins, but when it hit, the headpin leaped out of the pack, ricocheted off the sideboard, smacked the 4-pin, which bumped the wobbling 9-pin... and they all fell down.

That bit of luck reassured Allison. He calmly rolled two more balls into the pocket for his thirty-fifth and thirty-sixth consecutive strikes, for his third 300 game in a row, and the first 900 series in sanctioned competition.

Finally, Allison lost his composure. He fell to his knees and disappeared under a mob of well-wishers. When he emerged, there were tears in his eyes. One witness said, "There were a lot of tears in the eyes of grown men that night."

In order to be legitimate, a 300 game must be certified as such by the ABC. Immediately after Allison rolled his wonderful series, the ABC inspectors checked the surfaces of lanes 13 and 14 at La Habra 300 Bowl. Sadly, they came to the conclusion that the specifications that night were not in accordance with the rules of the ABC. They said that there was too much lane dressing, called *oil,* on the outside track of the boards of the lanes. Despite the fact that Allison did not use an outside track that night, which means that the improper lane preparation did not affect his game, the ABC was adamant. Allison's series was disallowed.

But the lack of official certification didn't affect the glory of Allison's achievement. A flurry of endorsement offers and interviews came his

way. "I even had an offer to tour the Far East," Allison said. Columbia Industries, the delighted manufacturers of the ball he used, bought it back from him for $3,000.00. It is displayed in a glass case in the lobby of Columbia's San Antonio factory and the company exhibits it frequently at trade shows and tournaments across the country.

Shortly after his historic night at La Habra 300 Bowl, Allison competed in the PBA Seniors tournament in Canton, Ohio. There he bowled five straight strikes to end his second game and then rolled twelve more in a row for another 300. "That showed them that the old pro can still roll those strikes," Glenn said.

When asked about returning to the PBA tour in earnest, 56-year-old Glenn said, "My legs can no longer tolerate the long grind of 42 games in three days under the stress of competition. That's why I'm in the liquor business and I intend to stay there. But I can still take off time for bowling exhibitions just the same. In a way I can have my cake and eat it too."

Allison faces the future calmly. If official immortality has been denied him, he is at least confident that his stature among bowling champions is assured. "The bowling world has accepted my 900," he said, "and I'm pleased with that. Though the ABC did not certify it, my 900 is something the world knows about. And, of course, I'll always know that I did it."

So do we, Glenn!

ANDY VARIPAPA

Andy Varipapa may not have been the greatest bowler of all time, but without doubt he was one of the best-known and most loved of the early champions. He must be given much of the credit for making bowling the popular sport it is today.

Andy could make the bowling bowl do unbelievable stunts. For years he toured the country as a representative of a bowling ball manufacturer and gave exhibitions of trick bowling that never ceased to wow the crowd. One of his best was bowling with two balls at the same time, rolling one left-handed so that it took out the 10-pin and the other right-handed so that it toppled the 7-pin. The balls crossed paths dangerously close at mid-lane, but Andy pulled off the stunt every time.

News of his talent filtered to Hollywood, and soon Andy had a contract to make a short film on bowling. He performed all his standard tricks for the camera plus a new one. Starlets in short dresses lined up straddling the far end of the lane. The 7-pin was set in its usual spot. Andy rolled his bowling ball through the tunnel of girls' legs and knocked down the 7-pin. It was vintage Hollywood and vintage Varipapa.

Andy had very little formal education, but had a great desire to educate himself all through his later life. He went to night school, took correspondence courses, and became a well-rounded, well-educated man. Before he began his bowling career, Andy was a machinist at the Brooklyn Navy Yard, and a good one. He said, "I realized early in life that second best is no good. You have to be the best or you're nobody."

Andy began to build his reputation as a bowler in the 1920s. At one time he averaged 207 pins for 90 games in 15 different bowling centers. Another time he averaged 212 for other outings of 150 games in different centers. These remarkable achievements were accomplished in the days before standardization of lane conditions. Unlike today, when lane conditions are controlled, the lanes one day might be oily and fast, on another day sticky and slow. Andy mastered them all.

This enthusiastic ambassador of bowling was never interested in the gambling side of the sport. He said, "I never cared for the gambling part of match play bowling. I really didn't want to take money from other bowlers and I didn't want them to take mine. I wanted to be paid for my bowling talent. I wanted guarantees because I wanted to earn money to support my family."

Andy put on exhibitions anywhere. In 1955 the owners of the Cincinnati Reds baseball team laid a single lane between third base and home plate just outside the baseline. Andy entertained the huge crowd before the game began. One new trick he developed for this event was that of rolling the ball down the lane by propelling it with the sole of his right shoe. Sure enough, he had one strike out of three tries as the crowd went wild.

Official records show that Andy rolled only one 300 game under tournament conditions, but Andy claimed to have rolled seventy-eight. The answer to this discrepancy probably lies in the fact that Andy gave so many bowling exhibitions. Often, while in the midst of bowling a game, Varipapa would roll consecutive strikes. He would ignore his previous score and begin counting from the point of his first strike as if it were a new game. If he then rolled twelve strikes in a row (no mean feat even then), he claimed a 300 game, one obviously not officially acceptable.

There is no doubt that Andy won the All-Stars event twice, once in 1946, when he was 55, and again in 1947. In the doubles with "Wrong Foot" Lou Campi he won the Bowling Proprietors Association doubles title in both 1947 and 1948. He was named Bowling Magazine All-American in 1948. When Andy was in his 60s, he rolled a 211 average for an entire season. At age 68, Andy was invited to bowl in the Phillies *Jackpot Bowling* television series. At first when his name was proposed to the producers of the program, they were dead set against having him bowl. They couldn't believe that a man that old could hold up under the hot lights and pressure of being watched by millions of people all over the country. Andy Varipapa, undisputed champion, rolled consecutive strikes to walk away with the $9,000 jackpot.

Allie Brandt, the diminutive bowler who holds the all-time high record

score of 886 for three games, once said, "Andy was one of the best who ever walked down a lane. He did more for the game than any other person, was a great competitor, and the finest advertisement I ever saw for the game."

Andy lived a long, happy life well into his 90s. Nobody really knew how old he was, not even Andy, because his parents, in the old fashioned way, refused to tell him his true birthdate. All of Andy's children received college educations. In his later years Andy said, "I love to sit at the family table and be surrounded by doctors and lawyers, scientists and teachers and know that I had something to do with instilling the need for learning in them."

EARL ANTHONY

Undoubtedly the greatest bowler who ever lived, Earl Anthony recently returned to "bowl a few tournaments" after having retired from an active professional bowling career after winning his forty-first PBA title and topping the one million dollar mark in prize money. What makes his achievements even more remarkable is the fact that this soft-spoken, modest gentleman did not pick up a bowling ball until he was twenty-one.

Before he discovered bowling, Earl Anthony played baseball for recreation, and after successfully pitching for one of the U.S. Air Force teams during his service, he seriously considered pursuing a professional baseball career. Eventually he decided he didn't quite have the talent to become a pro.

Earl married and moved to Tacoma, Washington. There he worked for a wholesale grocery company on the midnight shift. He did not earn a great deal of money, and sometimes it was hard to make ends meet.

Soon after Earl went to work, he was invited to join the company bowling league. Because he worked the graveyard shift, Earl bowled early in the morning. Right after work he grabbed a bite of breakfast and was on the lanes by 9 A.M. From the beginning Earl was something of a bowling oddity because he bowled left-handed. His co-workers kidded him, but that just made Earl more determined to improve his game.

In his first bowling season Earl averaged only 165, which was not bad for a beginner, but not good enough to win any of the pot games from the better bowlers in the league. He began practicing whenever he got the chance. Because bowling was expensive, it was Earl's good fortune to make friends with a lane owner who traded him a few free games for a little work around the lanes, generally setting up pins. Earl worked on perfecting his timing and his footwork. He "shadow bowled" (bowling without any pins set up), 20 to 25 games a day.

Soon Earl's bowling began to improve dramatically. In one year his average jumped to the 180s and in the next to the low 200s. His fellow bowlers, the ones who had been beating him regularly, were now losing the pot to the "left-hander." This pin money was very welcome in the Anthony household, for the first of their three children had arrived.

One day a professional bowling event came to town. Earl entered the tournament as an amateur in order to test himself against the pros. Although Earl finished out of the money, he had out-bowled more than one hundred other very good bowlers.

Now Earl had to decide for a second time in his life whether to go pro. He knew it was a financial risk, especially because he had a family to support, but he also knew he possessed a "secret" skill that very few bowlers were able to perfect. Most bowlers use the same arm-swing and approach speed, only adjusting their "line" to the pocket by varying the spot where they project the ball onto the lane. Earl's secret weapon was that he found a way to adjust his speed as well as his line to the pins. He is one of the few bowlers to do this successfully.

Earl's decision to become a pro is part of bowling history, underscored by the fact that he was named top professional bowler in 1974 and 1975 and elected to the PBA Hall of Fame in 1981.

A long and successful bowling career must be filled with wonderful stories, and Earl Anthony's years as King-of-the-Hill bowler are no exceptions. But there is one story which stands out among them all.

It happened at the time plastic bowling balls made their appearance. Their surface was so hard, the balls skidded on the lanes and were much less effective. One of the top bowlers, Don McCune, discovered that if he soaked his ball in a chemical solution, the ball softened. McCune's ball grabbed the lanes better after this treatment, and his score improved noticeably.

Other bowlers soon caught onto this trick. One night fourteen bowlers were staying in a motel in a small Illinois town during the course of a bowling tournament conducted by the PBA. The motel owner discovered that all the bowlers were soaking their balls in a bucketful of potentially flammable chemicals. He ordered each and everyone of them to "get those balls out of the motel."

The bowlers complied by grouping the pails together outside in the parking lot. A late-night driver, not expecting anything but cars in the lot, which was on a hill, ran right into the pails. Bang! Crash! Bowling Ball Thunder! All the lights in the motel flashed on and startled motel guests hurried to their windows to observe fourteen bowlers, some in their pajamas, some not, scrambling through the night to recover their precious bowling balls, some of which ended up more than two blocks away.

Earl says that a bowler will go to great lengths to get his special ball. He recalled one time when lane conditions in a mid-west tournament required an old rubber ball he had not used in years. Unfortunately, the ball he called "Old #37," was back in Tacoma in his basement. Urgently, he phoned his wife and told her to send it to him as fast as she could. She air-shipped it to him overnight at double the cost of the original ball. But Earl received it in time and used it well. He won the tournament.

There is a lot of drama in a professional sportsman's life, and for Earl Anthony the drama began in June 1978 as he prepared to bowl in a PBA tournament in San Jose, California. A jolt of pain shot through his chest. He ignored it, but it came back again even more intensely. He was in the throes of a serious heart attack. It was questionable he would survive, let alone ever bowl again.

But Earl recovered and slowly regained his strength. He walked miles a day to strengthen his legs and at last, with his doctor's permission, he began to bowl once more. In two months Earl made a remarkable comeback and was again ready for the professional tour. He went on to win 12 more PBA titles, including the National Championship in 1983.

After that accomplishment, Earl retired but three years later was lured back to the lanes starting with an event in Tacoma, Washington. He also owns and operates his own bowling establishment in Dublin, California. Sometimes he can be seen and heard as a television commentator for some of the bowling tournaments. His style, as ever, is modest, unassuming, and extremely knowledgeable. There can be no doubt in anyone's mind that Earl Anthony is a true champion.

CARMEN SALVINO

Carmen Salvino, now 42, is currently the "old man" of professional bowling. He was one of the bowlers of the PBA in 1959 and has to his credit the remarkable achievement of winning a major championship in each of four decades. He has won 18 major tournaments plus dozens more sponsored by other bowling organizations.

Carmen's reputation rests not only on his ability to knock down the pins in great quantity, but also in his talent as a showman. His body language, his gestures on the lanes, his piercing eyes, all add up to one of the most colorful performances by any bowler on the lanes today. He leaps, he spins, he poses. And his dialogue matches his actions. He will ask the crowd when a 10-pin refuses to fall, "Has anybody got a pistol? I'll shoot the rascal down!" (Only he doesn't say *rascal*.)

Salvino is an avid student of the phases of physical fitness that tailor his body for bowling. He said, "I wouldn't be able to average 213, the same average I had when I was 20, without being in shape. You'll never see me in one of those health clubs pumping iron. Bowlers don't need big, bunchy muscles like football players. We need flexibility and elongated muscles. I studied physiology, and I know.

"For my main exercise, I loop one end of a long, thick piece of rubber over a doorknob and the other end over an arm or a leg. Then I pull. Long sweeps. Lotsa times. I also do a lot of stretching and bending. A few years ago I could touch my palms to the floor without bending my knees. I can still get my knuckles down.

"I had back pains once, so I worked out a scale to measure body balance. I found out that my right leg was an eighth-inch shorter than my left one! I got a special shoe lift made, and it fixed me right up.

"Then there's the bowling itself. Most people see ten pins 60 feet away. I see an approach area that's different on every lane. I see an oily spot here, a dry spot there. I see pins that can vary in weight by as much as 5 ounces. I see the lines the other guys have bowled. I think of my footwork, the way I swing my arm, doing it the same every time. People who say bowling bores them don't see its complexities. At my level of the game, the complexities are what's important."

Salvino has studied the art and science of the bowling ball so intensely that he has invented a new one. He has a patent on a ball design that has two "weight blocks" instead of the usual one. Under ABC rules a bowling ball is permitted to be slightly out of perfect balance. That means one side may weigh up to one ounce more than its opposite side. There may be as much as a three-ounce difference between the top of the ball and the bottom of the ball. Where that weight is placed in the ball ultimately affects the way the ball curves or does not curve into the 1-3 pocket. A ball weighted on the left side toward the pins rather than toward the channel will hit the pins with more power than a ball not so weighted. (Note: That would be the left side of the ball rolled by a right-handed bowler, the right side by a left-handed bowler.)

Apparently Carmen has discovered that if a ball has two weight blocks inside it rather than the usual single weight block, the result is more strike-making power.

Carmen is working with a ball manufacturer and expects his new ball to be in mass production soon. He claims his ball will be revolutionary, the most stable ball ever made.

Carmen has delved deeply into the mathematics of bowling and has become an expert on the dynamic forces that cause bowling pins to go down when struck by a well-directed bowling ball. His studies led him to change his style dramatically. Salvino was originally a five-step bowler with a pushaway to get his ball in motion. Now he has no more pushaway and a much reduced swing pattern as he begins with the ball resting at arm's length dangling down his right side before he goes into a simplified four-step approach. At first his technique looked unorthodox, but now several players imitate it, notably Wayne Webb, who has been a tremendous success on the pro circuit.

Carmen's new style has resulted in greater achievements than ever before. Between 1973 and 1979 he averaged $40,000 a year in PBA prizes, winning tournaments in every year but one.

In 1984 Carmen turned fifty and became eligible for PBA Seniors

Competition. He wasted no time in winning his eighteenth title, leading the qualifying field by 515 pins and defeating Jimmy Schroeder in the championship 206-191 for the $15,000 first prize.

When Carmen has a bowling problem, he has moving pictures taken of his bowling style in action. A few years ago he got into a protracted slump. He said to one of his fellow bowlers, "The next time we have a break in the schedule I'm going home and look at my films."

Two weeks later, he was back on the tour and someone walked up to Salvino and asked if he'd seen anything on the film. To which Carmen responded, "Yes...I noticed that I'm losing more hair."

WAYNE WEBB

From earnings of $90 in 1975 and $1226 in 1976, Wayne Webb, "The Green Machine," has steadily pulled himself to the top level of modern professional bowlers. In 1980 he topped the $100,000 mark for the first time and followed that with two more great years $100,110 in 1984 and $127,993 in 1985. Already he has climbed into seventh position on the career money list with total earnings of $690,000 through 1985.

Webb, 29 years of age, is a diminutive bowler, 5-feet-5-inches tall, 145 pounds. His style is unorthodox. He dangles his bowling ball at his side, swinging it back and forth not unlike the way Carmen Salvino does. Then with a nod of his head as if to say, "Let's go," he starts off with a jerk and heads for the line in a bearlike shuffle. There he consistently delivers a vicious hook. Unorthodox bowler, yes, but orthodox money-winner because he has proved to be tough in the clutch, able to deliver the crucial strikes when he needs them.

Webb's father was a bowling proprietor in Rehoboth, Massachusetts, a small town with a population of only 6500. The bowling lane and the movie house were the centers of entertainment. With free bowling through the courtesy of his father, sometimes he would bowl as many as 40 to 50 games a day. How he developed his Salvino-like style no one knows, but practice of several hundred games a week brought his timing to near perfection. He started on the PBA tour in 1983, and was a first time winner that year, an unusual occurrence for a rookie.

Webb has out-bowled on many occasions such super stars as Mark Roth and Marshall Holman. For example, in 1980 he beat Roth, his main competitor, in four categories: earnings, titles (3), points, and games bowled. Webb was rewarded by being named Player of the Year. He has notified the bowling world that he intends to be named Bowler of the Decade and is slowly, but surely, building the record of victories that certainly will earn him consideration for that valuable title.

Webb is essentially a quiet young man, except for one notable trait. He always bowls in green clothing. His fellow competitors have nicknamed him the "Green Machine." Webb not only expresses the Green Machine theme in his clothing, but also in his bowling ball. Ebonite, the bowling equipment manufacturer that Webb has represented, designed a "Wayne Webb" bowling ball in solid green.

Webb might have been a professional baseball player, a catcher, if he had been an inch or two taller. But he has no regrets. He said, "I'm glad I took the bowling route. There are no height qualifications for throwing strikes. Look at Allie Brandt. He wasn't any bigger than I am and his record three-game score still stands after all these years." Brandt had an 886 total in 1939, and Webb is right, the record still stands.

After good seasons in 1981 and 1982, in which he earned $100,000 and $92,000, Wayne fell into what amounted to a slump for him in 1983. He limped along on earnings of only $43,000 and was most dissatisfied with his life and his bowling.

Then came a turning point in his mental attitude and as it turned out, his bowling career. He put on a tape of the movie *Flashdance.* He heard the young dancer's boyfriend tell her, "Go for the top of your profession." The message hit a nerve for Webb.

"I know what it's like not being there at the top. I was probably at the lowest point I've ever been in bowling. My attitude was bad. I was blaming the lanes, the bad breaks, everything but myself. I went back to work again on my bowling. When I was in the slump I wouldn't bowl at all except for the tournaments. I worked so hard to get there and then I suddenly stopped working as hard. I thought it was going to happen just by going out to the lanes."

Another factor in Webb's comeback happened by coincidence. He ran into Nelson Burton, Jr., in the Cleveland airport while the two bowlers were between flights. Bo told Wayne he had noticed that Wayne had stopped releasing the ball with the strength and force he had used in his meteoric climb to the top.

Burton said later, "What I told Webb was such a small thing but he's so young a bowler he might never have discovered his fault himself. The tip I gave him might help him to beat me some day, but I owe it to the game. Webb is a super talent." Burton's tip and Wayne's new attitude

and determination turned his year around. He won $23,000 at Chicago and in 1983 salvaged a $70,530 year.

Webb won back-to-back titles for the third time in his PBA career during the 1985 Winter Tour. The two victories brought Webb's total titles to 16. He surpassed the $100,000 mark for the fourth time in 1985, and with the 13 titles and the $600,000 he's earned in the 1980s alone, he leads all bowlers in this decade in both categories.

Despite these accomplishments, Webb feels he has not received the recognition he deserves. He appeared on seven televised bowling finals matches in 1985, and yet he is nowhere near as well known as Mike Aulby, who appeared on only two more. Wayne said, "I'm going to practice harder than I've ever practiced and force the respect and recognition from the public. I think it will happen, the respect, if the right people…those who have the power to promote me…help it to change."

Meanwhile, his record speaks for itself. Webb's prediction that he will be named Bowler of the Decade just may come true.

NELSON BURTON, JR.

Darkly handsome, trim and athletic, Nelson Burton, Jr., glows with the aura of success in the bowling field and in life in general. He is the son of Nelson Burton, who is generally regarded as one of the greatest match play bowlers of the 1930s and 1940s. Nelson, Sr., bowled in the St. Louis area with such bowling greats as Don Carter, Tom Hennessey, Pat Patterson, and the colorful Harry Smith.

Nelson Burton, Jr.'s nickname, Bo, came from the inability of his younger brothers to pronounce the word *brother.* Bo practically grew up with a bowling ball in his hand. When he was only five, he was the tiny star of Junior Bowling in the St. Louis leagues, rolling a light-weight but full size ball for many strikes. Bo officially started his bowling career as a Junior Bowler. At the age of 16 he rolled his first 300 game. He now has seven sanctioned 300 games to his credit along with eight other almost-300s of 299 and 298.

Bo Burton has had a remarkable career starring in two fields, first as a professional bowler, and in recent years as an outstanding sports television commentator.

After a stint in the U.S. Army, Bo came back to school at St. Louis University. While there he began to work seriously on his bowling game. In 1964, he ventured out into the jungle of the PBA tour, a lamb going to the slaughter, for rarely does a new bowler succeed quickly. However, he became an immediate success, winning his first title that summer at Louisville. In 1965 he became the idol of the PBA when he appeared on the nationally televised finals of six out of the eleven tournaments he entered on the winter tour, finishing second four times.

The famous bowler Billy Welu was at that time the bowling expert who was helping Chris Schenkel announce the televised PBA finals on the ABC network. Welu died suddenly of a heart attack and Bo was offered the chance to take Welu's place. He did the job so well that since 1975 he has been the regular announcer along with Schenkel on *The Pro Bowlers Tour*. Three times he has been nominated as "Best Color Analyst" on the show, which has been number one in its time slot for 10 consecutive years regardless of competition on the other networks.

There have been many highlights in Bo's bowling career. He has won no less than nine individual singles, doubles (with partners Dave Soutar and his own brother Neil), and team titles in the ABC tournament Classic Division from 1965 to 1979. His best showing was his 2079 for nine games in the All-Events in 1979, an astronomical 231 average for a bowler who has to cross many unfamiliar, brand-new lanes. Bo has had eleven 800 series, with a high of 869, a 289.6 average. He holds the highest lifetime average of any bowler in ABC history.

In the finals of the Hammer Open, on February 11, 1984, Bo shattered a 12-year-old PBA record by rolling 1050 for four games on the nationally televised finals in Florissant, Missouri. He had qualified in the fourth slot for the TV matches and opened with a 278-218 victory over Paul Gibson, but he still faced formidable opponents in Marshall Holman, Pete Couture, and top-seeded Pete Weber. Moreover, Weber was bowling on his home lanes and was a heavy favorite to win.

Burton walloped Holman 279 to 217. Then, needing a tenth frame double to edge Couture, he got the important strike, winning 257 to 249. The Weber match turned out to be an easy one as Bo rolled 236 to Pete's 184. Bo's series, a 262 average per game, surpassed the old record of 255, which had been held by Larry Laub since 1972.

The highlight of his career, Bo said, came in 1981 when he joined his father in the ABC Hall of Fame. He was the youngest player to be so honored. The Burton duo are the only father-son bowlers ever elected into the Hall of Fame.

At a bowling clinic recently Burton was discussing the turning point in his career. He said, "When I first got out onto the Tour, I simply collapsed as I got close to winning a tournament. Six times in a row I made the televised finals and every time I choked. Then, I happened to run into that great old-time bowling champion, Hank Marino. I told him about my trouble and asked his advice. Here's what he told me: 'When you get into that crucial tenth frame, you probably look up after you roll the ball, not watching to see that it hits your target line. Here's your answer. Keep

your eye on your spot until the roar of the crowd tells you that your ball has hit the pocket.' That was the cure. From then on I never choked again. I didn't always win, but I gave it my best shot."

Bo was recently asked about his most embarrassing moment on TV. He said, "When I first started to help Chris Schenkel with the telecasts, we would begin the show with his asking me who I thought might be the eventual winner. One time when the lanes were really soft and the scoring was good in the preliminary rounds, I made the prediction that the scores in the finals would be unusually high. Imagine my embarrassment when the two finalists rolled into splits and made miss after miss for games in the 150s and 140s. I died with every split. It taught me a good lesson not to predict the outcome of a bowling match because anything can happen and usually does."

Bo and his wife, Sissy, recently bought and operate a farm thirty miles west of St. Louis. The Burtons have four children, two daughters, a son, and a baby boy.

Bo raises oats, wheat, soybeans and corn and has livestock herds, which are pure bred Black Angus. Not long ago he bought the top Black Angus bull at the University of Missouri spring auction. He has high hopes for the future of his cattle operation. Nelson Burton, Jr., great bowler, excellent television announcer, and now gentleman farmer, is a man who understands the meaning of success.

DONNA ADAMEK

She's only five-feet-two-inches tall. You'd never guess that Donna Adamek could roll one of the most devastating hooks in the history of women's bowling. That's why this twenty-nine-year-old champion is called the Mighty Mite.

Donna is the youngest of four children and grew up in Monrovia, California, which has a population of 30,015 and one four-lane, antiquated bowling alley where the pins are still being set by a seventy-eight-year-old human pin-setter. One day when she was ten years old, Donna went bowling with her parents. Her father was a 165-average bowler at that time and her mother was in the 140 range. To their great surprise, tiny Donna out-bowled them right from the start. On her fourth game she rolled a score of 200. Although she didn't realize it then, her future as a champion bowler was already foreordained.

Although she is a natural left-hander, Donna started to bowl right-handed because she couldn't find a house ball to fit her, and she used her right-handed mother's ball. She added, "Besides, there were very few left-handed bowlers where I grew up and there was a feeling that left-handers were oddities. That's why I continued to bowl right-handed. Furthermore, I was scoring well, too. Why should I change?"

Donna bowled for fun throughout her youth. She went to California State College at age 18. But the attraction of the game of bowling and the lure of the dollars on the Ladies Professional Tour was too great. After a year of college she left to become a professional bowler.

Within a year she led all the women professional bowlers with an average of 207. The next year she again was high-average bowler at 203. Exhibitions and endorsements began to come her way. In 1979 she earned $30,000 from outside activities alone.

Donna rolled a 15½-pound ball for the first few years of her professional career, but has recently gone to a 15-pounder, claiming she can

be more accurate with it covering her spaces. She said, "I don't think I've lost any strikes, either." She owns no less than 100 bowling balls, which are supplied to her by her sponsor, Columbia Industries. She wears out a ball every two or three weeks. Because of differences in lane conditions (the amount of oil used on dressing the individual lanes varies from a great deal to very little), Donna customarily carries a half dozen balls with her on the road. She has a customized van that she drives to many tournaments.

Donna has won more than 250 trophies in her short but very successful career. She has given most of them away to schools so they can use them, with newly engraved nameplates, for their own champions in bowling. Recently Donna bought a condominium with her winnings, and there she displays her most beautiful trophies.

When Donna is on the road, she finds a good motel and watches soap operas on TV. She also relaxes by working at wood-turning. Donna practices one to two hours every morning under the supervision of Tosh Kinjo, an excellent Japanese bowler and teacher. Donna said, "I guess I'm a loner, but you don't see any of the girls who are serious about winning out dancing the night before a tournament."

Her diligence undeniably has paid off. By the end of the 1985 season Donna Adamek earned more money in her career than any other female bowler in history. She had a total of $218,734. Adamek is already seventh on the all-time earnings list and will probably climb higher in the future, considering her youth and exceptional bowling talent.

DICK WEBER

Dick Weber's winning record spans twenty-four years, from his first PBA victories in Paramus and Dayton in 1959 to the Senior Championship in Canton in 1983. His blonde hair is silver now, but his flashing smile and winning ways are still the same. This slim man, weighing about 150 pounds and standing five-foot-ten inches, is one of the greatest bowlers of all time.

Badly bitten by the bowling bug when he was a teenager, Dick Weber worked at many different jobs to finance his passion for the game. He was a mailman, a milkman, and a screw machine operator. Weber said, "I even delivered groceries on the weekends. I did anything that would allow me to bowl my five nights a week and bowl my pot games."

Right about the time Dick was grooming his game, the late fifties, St. Louis, Chicago, Detroit, Cleveland, Minneapolis, and Milwaukee were the breeding grounds for the greatest bowlers and the best five-man bowling teams. The Classic League bowlers of St. Louis became interested in Dick and he was asked to join the famous Budweiser Beer team. When Dick joined, the other members were Don Carter, Ray Bluth, Billy Welu, all three of whom are in the PBA Hall of Fame, and Tom Hennessey, who deserves to be there. This star-studded team shot a record score of 3858 pins, an average of 257 pins per game per man for 15 games in the March 1961 ABC tournament. This record, in all conceivable probability, will never be surpassed.

Just as Earl Anthony was smoothness in action from the left side of the lane, Dick Weber was the ultimate in smoothness from the right. It seemed he could do anything he wanted to do with a bowling ball. He could line an almost straight ball into the pocket from the corner. He could crank out the biggest bender from the center of the lane. And he had every shot in between. Once Dick found his line there was no stopping the many strikes that usually ensued.

The biggest thrill for Weber was not a long string of strikes, however, but converting a wide open spare such as the 6-7-10. He explained, "The odds against it are very high and your ball has to cross from 10 to 30 boards in order to make the conversion.

"Of course, getting a big string of strikes is a thrill for anyone. I've never made the 7-10 split, however. If I ever did, that would be the biggest thrill of all."

In addition to winning tournaments, Dick represented the American Machine and Foundry Company, a bowling equipment manufacturer. AMF sent Dick, his four children, and his wife on a 35,000 mile trip around the world. He also conducted demonstrations of bowling technique, using AMF products, of course, on the home front, even in the center of a rodeo arena during intermission. As the product competition grew, AMF's promotion campaigns became more outlandish. Weber bowled, on an AMF lane, against the women's champion Silvia Wene in a jet airplane—in flight. Weber even bowled (?) against an archer, Charlie Davis, who shot arrows at the head-pin while Dick rolled his bowling ball. If Davis hit the headpin, he got a strike, if he missed, a spare. Davis won, Dick recalled.

Recently Dick was diagnosed as suffering from a rare disease. Fortunately this early discovery followed by successful treatment has put Dick back on the road to health and strength.

"I said a few years ago I was going to bowl until I was eighty-six and then retire. I thought I would bowl forever. But I had a lot of time to think after that operation. I guess it won't bother me to retire a bit early. I'm burned out, I guess. I get tired of thinking about bowling, thinking about the proper line, and trying to keep my concentration. There are times when I just want to lay it aside for however long I can get away from it. I just want to forget bowling other than working at my own bowling lanes. Oh, I'd bowl a couple of tournaments here or there. It's great to be a 'has-been.' I'll tell you, I've never been happier in all my life."

He went on to say, "When you're sick you've got a lot of time to think about dying. I hope to die in a bowling lane with my bowling shoes on. Just don't leave that 10-pin beside me, that's all!"

Dick's youngest son Pete has followed in his father's footsteps and successfully wears his bowling shoes. A professional bowler, Pete's career is coming along nicely. The Weber legacy will live for a long time.

EDDIE ELIAS

If you watch the professional bowlers on ABC television on Saturday afternoons, you will often see the camera pan across the spectators. If you look closely at the front row you frequently will see a handsome dark-haired man dressed in a dark suit and wearing a conservative tie. He is Eddie Elias, the man who started professional bowling on its way to the tremendous success it now is.

It all began twenty-seven years ago when Don Carter, Basil "Buzz" Fazio, Dick Hoover, and several other great bowlers of that time complained to Eddie that professional golfers were getting lots of prize money and why didn't pro bowlers get some, too? From that suggestion the Professional Bowlers Association was formed: thirty-four male bowlers who bowled in three tournaments the following year for prize money of $49,500. Today nearly three thousand professional bowlers compete in fifty-five national tournaments and one-hundred-and-twenty-five regional tournaments for prize money that exceeds $5,000,000. Earl Anthony, Mark Roth and Marshall Holman, modern day champions have each earned more than $1,000,000 in prize money, not to mention additional "unofficial" income from sponsorship of products such as bowling balls and other equipment.

Eddie Elias, a native of Akron, Ohio, is well-built, standing six-feet-two-inches tall. He was a good athlete in his own right on the Akron All-City basketball team in 1946. He attended the University of Akron and there earned letters in baseball as well as in basketball. He was named to the Who's Who in American Colleges, an indication that his talents were recognized early in his career. Although he might have gone on to a baseball career, he chose to become an attorney. He graduated from Western Reserve Law School in 1956 and later on earned a doctorate in law as well. For a while, Eddie went into the radio and television field as a performer and producer of programs in Akron and Cleveland. It was then that the fortuitous meeting with Carter, Fazio, and Hoover occurred. Eddie had the foresight to realize that if he could interest the television networks in his newly founded organization, there might be money enough for a substantial increase in the bowlers' income. Since then all the major networks have regularly televised bowling events and important tournaments. Anybody who had one of the first TV sets remembers *Make That Spare* and *Jackpot Bowling.* Chances are, anyone who ever owned a TV set has caught a glimpse of *Pro Bowlers Tour,* which has been running for 29 years.

Elias has received many awards recognizing his important contributions to the success of modern bowling. In 1961 he was honored by *National Bowling Illustrated* for "outstanding contributions to the advancement of bowling" and in 1965 was given the BPAA award, (Bowling Proprietors Association of America) which Jackie Gleason and J. Edgar Hoover had won before him.

Once he had put the PBA on a solid profitable footing, Eddie branched out into other fields, including merchandising and promotion of sports. His company handles the business affairs of golfers such as "Chi Chi" Rodriguez, Frank Urban "Fuzzy" Zoeller, Hubert Green, John Mahaffey, Ken Venturi, bowling's Don Carter, Dick Weber, Nelson Burton, Jr., Carmen Salvino, and TV personalities Marlo Thomas and Phil Donahue.

Elias earned the 1968 New York Sportscasters Award for Man of the Year and he was elected to the Professional Bowlers Association Hall of Fame in 1968. Also, he was inducted into the American Bowling Congress Hall of Fame as well in 1985.

Eddie says that the greatest and most exciting moment in his career happened when he was able to persuade the Firestone Rubber Company to put up $100,000 for the first Tournament of Champions, an event which has come to rival the importance of the National Open in golf. "It was in 1965 and up to that time $2,500 to $10,000 was the most we could get in additional money for prizes. Incidentally the amount is up to $500,000 now." Eddie also says that he always gets a big thrill when he attends the final matches of the PBA.

"One time I got so excited that when the match was over I congratulated the guy who lost. Weber had beaten Don Carter and I hugged

Carter. Weber just smiled and told me he was going to teach me how to
keep score!"

The next time you watch the PBA televised matches see if you can find Eddie in that front row of spectators., He'll be there with his beautiful wife alongside him, cheering the bowlers in the final frames of his own brain child.

MIKE AULBY

$\mathbf{M}$ike Aulby is only 26 years old and has already been named Player of the Year 1985 by the *Sporting News.* Mike's success story is truly a remarkable one. He's not tall, only five-feet-seven-inches in height, not big and burly like some of the other bowling muscle men, weighs only 145 pounds. He wears rimless wraparound aviator glasses. You'd never guess that this quiet, unassuming gentleman rolls such a devastating hook from the left side of the lane in the same track Earl Anthony used so long and so well. In fact, it is entirely possible that Mike will be the next Earl Anthony on the tour if he is not already the reincarnation of that great champion bowler. Earl himself said, "Mike Aulby's potential is unlimited."

Aulby grew up in Indianapolis and still lives there in a house bought with his winnings. His father was a glazier, a cutter and installer of glass. Mike played baseball when he was young and was a hero to his teammates because he could call upon his Dad to fix any windows broken by foul balls or extra long drives over the fence.

When Mike was ten, his oldest sister, Peggy, let him tag along with her when she bowled at Playbowl Lanes in Indianapolis. By the time Mike was sixteen he rolled *six* 300 games in a space of six months.

"Without junior bowling, I probably wouldn't be where I am today," Mike says. "I joined a league the next year and I couldn't wait until Saturday to come so I could bowl my three games. By my freshman year at Franklin Central High I had a job at Playbowl doing cleanup or whatever needed to be done. I just wanted to be around bowlers and I could bowl for only twenty-five cents a game, Playbowl had the best junior program in the city. In the ninth grade I was competing in three leagues and by my senior year I was bowling in six leagues every week. The Youth Bowlers traveling league really helped my game. It was a big break for me...taught me how to read the lanes." In 1978 Mike won the Indiana state title in the All-American Youth Championships.

One Halloween night soon afterward Mike nearly was taken out of the bowling scene for good. His car was smashed by a train at a crossing and Mike had to have 60 stitches in his head. Despite his injuries, he bowled a week later with his head still swathed in bandages.

Mike joined the tour in 1979 and that first year in a head-to-head confrontation with his idol, Earl Anthony, at the PBA National tournament, Mike emerged the victor. He was on his way, he thought.

Although he was third on the money list in 1983, he ran into a serious slump soon afterward. He said, "I hated the traveling and being alone so much. It affected my bowling." Then love struck Mike and straightened out his life, it seems. When he was bowling in California he met Tami Canepa. Her father runs the Saratoga, California, lanes, so Tami was right at home in the bowling scene. Marriage to Tami helped Mike regain his form and desire to excel. He proceeded to win his first tournament in three years and finished fourth that year in earnings.

On the lanes Aulby is loose and limber. He holds the ball in front of him as if he is caressing it gently before he starts his four careful steps to the line. The ball is curled a bit behind him just prior to the release in a long, liquid flowing action. His ball seems to break a bit more than Anthony's. It sometimes barely misses the channel on the left on its way down the lane, but once past that danger his ball simply explodes at the pocket, smashing the pins sideways with awesome power. Aulby's delivery is so well balanced that he is able to hold his pose on his right foot like a ballet dancer and stay there for the few seconds it takes for the ball to strike the pocket. He's no showboat like Marshall Holman, but he can and does flash a sweet smile when he knows his game is on.

Aulby and Steve Cook, another excellent bowler in the modern scene, are married to sisters. The brothers-in-law made quite a pair as they won the PBA Doubles Classic in June 1985, splitting the $25,000 first prize money. Cook, who is known as "The Cookie Monster," is a mere six-feet-seven-inches tall and nearly 300 pounds in weight. A full foot shorter, Mike was the true Jeff in this Mutt and Jeff combination.

The climax of Aulby's 1985 season came when he won the final tournament of the year at Saginaw, Michigan. All Mike had done in 1985 was capture six titles and smash Earl Anthony's single season money mark of $164,735. Mike cracked the $200,000 barrier and was the landslide winner of the Bowler of the Year Award.

DON CARTER

Don Carter has one of the outstanding records in bowling history. There is no doubt that he would have been in the million dollar class in earnings had he been bowling in the modern era. But at age 60, after four knee operations, Don has retired from active bowling. His accomplishments, however, are enough to fill several careers.

Six times he was named Bowler of the Year by the Bowling Writers of America (1953, '54, '57, '58, '60 and '62). He was declared All American by the *Bowlers Journal* eleven times, from 1951 through 1963, an all-time record. He was the first man to roll three successive 1900 series in the ABC Tournament (1951, '52 and '53). He had five consecutive 1800 series in the ABC (1950-1954). He has had twenty-three 300 games, thirteen of them in non-sanctioned open play. With two differently named teams, but essentially the same bowlers, he won two Classic Team and one All-Events titles in 1953 (with Pfeiffer Brewing) and in 1962 (with Carter Gloves).

Before he started his spectacular career, Carter was an all-around sports star at Wellston High School in St. Louis. At six-foot-one, he played in the infield and pitched. He had a short span in Class D Minor League baseball with the Red Spring team in North Carolina, a farm team of the Philadelphia Phillies.

Carter said, "I might never have been a bowler at all if I had been able to hit a curve ball. When I couldn't, that was the end of it. I started to bowl. I was twenty-three years old."

Carter's rise to prominence in the bowling world was slow. At first he bowled in orthodox fashion, with his right arm straight and firm in both back- and forward swing and release. He was, at that time, a good bowler, but not any better than hundreds, perhaps thousands of others who were bowling 200 averages in "scratch," that is, no handicap, leagues all over the United States. Then he had what turned out to be the fortunate misfortune of having a cyst develop in the palm of his bowling hand. For a while he could not bowl at all. The cyst healed, but scar tissue had formed. When he resumed bowling, Carter found that he had pain in his palm when he attempted to "lift" the ball, closing his fingers at the delivery point. Most good bowlers' hand action is not unlike that of snapping the fingers, the fingers closing quickly on the hand after the ball is released.

To help ease the pain, he experimented with pushing the ball instead of snapping it out with a closed palm. He also decided to crook his right elbow in his backswing to help him accomplish the push. The combination of push plus the bent elbow proved miraculous for Carter. He developed an uncannily effective strike ball. His style was decidedly unorthodox, but it worked for him and brought him head and shoulders above the other bowlers of his day.

Although tall, Carter is moderately hunch-backed with a pronounced curve forward at his upper spine. This gave him a unique approach. He crouched over, carrying his whole body fairly low to the floor, and shuffled up to the line with four extremely precise steps. Then at the line he did everything right with his push delivery. He stayed with the ball, that is, stayed down to the line, and delivered an extraordinarily accurate but surprisingly gentle ball.

Using this technique, he developed the knack of getting into the 1-3 pocket from behind the 1-pin. That meant very little power was wasted on the head-pin and the ball could get into the heart of the pins, hit the 5-pin, the "Kingpin," and cause strikes. Another benefit of Carter's delivery was that it kept him almost immune to the dreaded 10-pin tap, which is a good hit that fails to topple the 10-pin. He became famous for what was called the *tickler* or *love tap* hit in which the 6-pin comes off the sideboard and strokes the 10-pin down as if it were tickling it.

Carter was kidded a lot about his bowling style. In defense of his slow ball he said, "I find rolling the ball with speed is a detriment. The pins fly out of position without getting a chance to mix thoroughly when you throw the ball into them too hard. I emphasize control rather than power. I use a three-finger ball with a semi-fingertip drilling. I bend my elbow because it works for me. I don't care what people think. You can look at my record."

Despite its undeniable success, Carter's bowling style was so unortho- dox that no one since his time has ever attempted to imitate it.

Carter said the highlight of his career happened when he and his Budweiser team set the new team record of 3858 in the Classic Team division of the ABC. "Can you imagine bowling on a team that had Ray Bluth shooting two 267s and a 300? No wonder we broke the record."

When Carter was actively bowling, he successfully promoted the first bowling glove, which had a padded palm to help keep the bowler's hand in proper position on the side of the ball. This came to be known as the Don Carter glove. Now Don helps to promote ten different bowling lanes in Florida, Louisiana and Texas. He and his wife tour in their motor home, chauffeur-driven by Billy Panasuk, a long-time bowling friend of Don's, whose knee troubles keep him from driving. In Miami, the Carters have a new home, a tennis court, and a swimming pool. "Life is not too bad," said Don, "but I'd give anything for some good knees so I could bowl again."

NED DAY

Edward P. "Ned" Day (1911-1971) was the first true stylist in bowling technique. His smooth and rhythmic delivery paid off handsomely. Until he came along in the bowling world, the main idea of the bowlers was to throw, not roll, the ball as hard as possible at the pins and knock them down through sheer force. Day realized that a smooth, unforced delivery would be more successful in the long run. Today he is known as bowling's first great champion.

Although he was born in Los Angeles, Ned Day began his bowling career in the Milwaukee Classic leagues. He was captain of the famous national champion team sponsored by the Heil Brewery. Day was best known for his individual match play. Five times he defended his national title successfully. He bowled in 28 straight ABC tournaments starting in 1930 and carried a 200 lifetime ABC average. In 1948 he was the ABC All-Events champion, which means that his average in the singles, doubles, and team event was the highest of all the thousands of bowlers who bowled in the ABC that year.

Under that banner of the Tavern Pales, another beer company sponsor who made a popular beer in the Wisconsin-Illinois area, Ned bowled with the "Boomer," Buddy Bomar, another super-star of bowling at that time. The two great bowlers won many head-to-head matches against the best opponents in the country. Toward the end of his career Ned bowled for the Falstaff team out of Chicago. That team won the ABC tournament team title in 1956.

Ned was a clean-cut fellow, handsome, 5-feet-11-inches tall, slim, always in fine physical shape as a result of a regular exercise program. Ned was a gentleman at all times, gracious and helpful to the many bowlers who bowled against him, and the fans who besieged him with questions at the numerous clinics he conducted for the Brunswick company, which kept him on the payroll for years as their goodwill ambassador. When Ned finally was unable to bowl, he told Brunswick that he could not continue to represent the company. They wanted him whether he could bowl or not, but he felt he would be misrepresenting himself if he did, so he turned down their offer in spite of the money they offered.

He was an excellent public speaker, much in demand at sporting functions, which brought him to the attention of the Hollywood film makers. They summoned Ned west where he made several successful movie shorts on bowling. While there he met the famous comedy actor, Harold Lloyd, who liked what he saw in Ned. Lloyd suggested that they go into business together. Lloyd put up the money for a large bowling establishment, which Day fronted and operated. Famous bowler Hank Marino also participated in the project. As a result, the lanes were named Lo-Da-Mar. The venture was most successful and soon many of Hollywood's starlets simply "had to be seen" at Lo-Da-Mar lanes.

Day was one of the first famous bowlers to write an instruction book on the sport. With the help of a knowledgeable sportswriter as his ghost, Day produced the first sports instruction book to use sequence photography. *How To Bowl* showed every step, every move of the famous Day delivery. The book was a big success and sold for years. Today it is a classic and sells for many times its original price in the out-of-print book market.

Day had an interesting idiosyncrasy. He never shook hands with anyone for fear that someone might crush his bowling hand. He dodged the hand-shake cleverly by telling the fans, "I ran into some poison ivy the other day so we'd better not shake hands today." The line lasted him a lifetime.

Day gave up competitive bowling in the mid-1950s. Although he had not been under pressure for years, he agreed in 1959 to be part of a TV bowling series, *Championship Bowling.* He rose to the occasion, defeated such younger stars as Don Carter and Tom Hennessey, and recorded one last major triumph.

In August, 1970, Day was chosen a member of the All-Time (Pre-1950) American Bowling Congress team.

Ned Day's widow is alive at the age of 74 and lives in Florida. She recalled her husband being the "fashion plate" of bowling. He had dozens of bowling outfits and dozens of tailored suits. "I remember him practicing his delivery in the basement in our recreation room. He had a metronome and a taped line on the floor. He would walk it for hours perfecting his timing. I remember, too, when he had his bowling gold medal made into a fob for his grandfather's watch. He always wore it in the right hand pocket of his bowling trousers. I suppose the sight of it was meant to intimidate his opponents."

Mrs. Day said that Ned had a bad fall from a ladder in the late 1950s and broke his ankle. He never could bowl again.

In the last years of his life, Ned Day operated a book store. You can be sure that *How To Bowl* was for sale there.

INDEX